Bullies of Woke
and their
Assault on Mental Health

Bullies of Woke
and their
Assault on
Mental Health

Diane Weber Bederman

Published by New English Review Press
a subsidiary of World Encounter Institute
PO Box 158397
Nashville, Tennessee 37215
&
27 Old Gloucester Street
London, England, WC1N 3AX

Cover Art and Design by Kendra Mallock

ISBN: 978-1-943003-63-1

Library of Congress Control Number: 2022937762

First Edition

NEW ENGLISH REVIEW PRESS
newenglishreview.org

To my father Abraham and my mother Sarah,
to my children and grandchildren
and all who follow,
and always, Marc.

Of all tyrannies, a tyranny sincerely exercised for the good of its victims may be the most oppressive. It would be better to live under robber barons than under omnipotent moral busybodies. The robber baron's cruelty may sometimes sleep, his cupidity may at some point be satiated; but those who torment us for our own good will torment us without end for they do so with the approval of their own conscience. —C.S Lewis

Second-century A.D. skeptic philosopher Sextus Empiricus noted, eventually the truth emerges and cosmic justice is rendered: *The millstones of the gods grind late, but they grind fine.*

Contents

Preface

I AM WRITING this book to give courage to our parents and grandparents and our politicians, no matter race, colour, creed or sexual orientation, to fight back and protect our children, our families, our communities and our countries from the bullying by the new religion of Progressivism and their apostles of fear. Their constant bullying is destroying Western culture and affecting the mental well-being of our children that can last generations.

Introduction

Civilizations die from suicide, not by murder.
—Arnold Toynbee

M ANY MAY ASK: why write about wokeness, critical race theory, progressive ideology, and cancel culture? How many people really believe in it, anyway? Does it matter? Do ideologies need a large contingent of people to change the world view of the majority? How many people were needed to create America? The Boston Tea Party plunged America into a revolutionary war to break away from Britain and her culture. How many were involved?

In Rwanda, Hutus and Tutsis went after each other with machetes. In just 100 days in 1994, about 800,000 people were slaughtered. The slaughter was initiated by a small group of ethnic Hutu extremists who were targeting members of the minority Tutsi community, as well as their political opponents, irrespective of their ethnic origin.

And though I dislike referring so often to WWII and Germany, Germany was considered the most enlightened nation in the world, boasting great authors, philosophers and creators. How many Nazis were needed to get Hitler installed? And then, without a sound of dissent the Nazis developed a military industrial complex for the sole purpose of murdering people who did not fit in with their idea of the ideal Aryan.

In other words, world views can be changed by a small

group of dedicated people who believe in their mission and proselytize to the point of bullying.

The Progressives, with their cancel culture, Critical Race Theory, and never-ending bullying will change the West, and America in particular, if the adults in the room, parents and grandparents do not get involved, learn about the ideology, and fight back.

Why should you read this book? Who am I to talk about the Progressive value system, bullying and mental illness?

First, let's talk about mental illness. I was diagnosed at age fifty with chronic recurrent depression. Looking back, I developed depression and anxiety when I was thirteen. I can remember the anxiety attack vividly. I have had my fair share of therapy that greatly helped me. As an adult, I started to write about mental illness on my blog, dianebederman.com, and I wrote and narrated a six part radio series, "The Many Voices of Mental Illness."[1]

When I was eight years old, I was bullied by my school principal. I also remember that vividly. And I caved in. As for Progressive ideology, I have studied it closely for many years. I am a hospital chaplain and have studied ethics and came to believe that the only ethic, the only value system that makes life free, is the Judeo-Christian ethic that underpins our constitutions, particularly in America. I wrote a book about that ethic entitled, *Back to the Ethic: Reclaiming Western Values.*[2] The Progressives seem adamantly opposed to our basic Judeo-Christian values. They are also against the traditional family. Now, I have lots of experience with the traditional family. I am the mother of three and grandmother of nine.

We have lived through something like this before.

The McCarthy years are looked upon as a dark era in American history. So many lives were ruined in a "witch hunt."[3]

---

1 See: https://dianebederman.com/podcasts/.

2 Diane Weber Bederman, *Back to the Ethic: Reclaiming Western Values,* Mantua Books, 2015.

3 See: Diane Weber Bederman, "Memories of the McCarthy Years: The return of blacklisting," *The Bederman blog,* April 9, 2019.

Senator McCarthy spent almost five years trying in vain to expose communists and other left-wing "loyalty risks" in the U.S. government. Then later, McCarthy's increasingly wild accusations were so intimidating that few people dared to speak out against him.[4]

Sound familiar?

We in the West have taken freedom for granted. We have become a frightened people. We succumb to fear—fear of being ridiculed, shamed, called out for being noncompliant. We even have to fear for our livelihoods. We have allowed ourselves to be cowed and silenced by ideologies that are diametrically opposed to our own moral system. We have been so inclusive that we have tolerated values that call for the death of our civilization. Where will it end?

---

4 See: Joseph MCarthy, *History.com*, October 29, 2009. https://www.history.com/topics/cold-war/joseph-mccarthy.

1

Beware Progressive Bullies
Attacking our Western Values

Without ideas held in common there is no common action, and without common action, there may still be men, but there is no social body. In order that society should exist and, a fortiori, that a society should prosper, it is necessary that the minds of all citizens should be rallied and held together by certain predominant ideas.

—Alexis de Tocqueville, *Democracy in America,* 1831.

W E ARE HELD TOGETHER by common shared morals, values, ethics, and stories.

In America, these predominant ideas come from the Judeo/Christian ethic that the Founding Fathers used as the foundation for America's Constitution.

The American Declaration of Independence incorporated the eighteenth-century ideas of John Locke and Gottfried Wilhelm Leibniz about the God-given freedom of the individual: "We hold these truths to be self-evident, that all men are created equal, that they are endowed by their Creator with certain unalienable Rights that among these are Life, Liberty and the Pursuit of Happiness."

The most important pillars of that Constitution rest on the idea that all people are born with equal intrinsic value, all life

16

is sacred and we have free will. Seems simple enough. But it isn't simple. Especially the concept of free will. Western culture and ethical monotheism have transformed the world. And the world's greatest transformation has been the knowledge that we humans are individually accountable for our actions. We choose our paths; they are not chosen for us. We are subjects of our destiny and not objects of our fate. Victimhood is not part of the American ethic or Constitution.

We had raised generations of young people on these values, which became enmeshed in their DNA; what Richard Dawkins refers to as cultural memes. They were our guiding light.

What happens when that guiding light is dimmed, or extinguished?

What happens to those cultural memes, that culturally acquired sense of self?

I am going to share with you a story from *The Twilight Zone*. It was a television series in the early 1960's written and hosted by Rod Serling. He never shied away from looking at cultural norms.

Many years ago, Rod Serling wrote an episode ("Eye of the Beholder") about a beautiful young woman who kept asking the doctors to help her, fix her, make her more like all the others. We watch as the doctors and nurses perform surgery after surgery, but to no avail. They cannot repair her. She falls apart and is taken to a place with others just like her. Then we glimpse the doctors and nurses -- the normal people. They have faces of pigs. The beautiful girl is the opposite of "normal."

The doctors and nurses represent cancel culture, which undermines the traditional family, the education system and the concept of the nation-state itself. Everything we know to be true is under attack to the point that our children think they need to look like the doctors and the nurses rather than the young lady. Their world is being torn asunder; their assumptions and life experiences are questioned at an early age and that can lead to mental illness.

Wokeness, Critical Race Theory, and cancel culture combine to create a new culture that has nothing in common with the individual liberty enshrined in the Constitution. These ideas have been circulating since the early 1940s but were never so well promoted as now, when these "doctors and nurses" have invaded education, politics and media. Never have children been faced with such diametrically opposed value systems, such that the tension between them will affect their mental well-being, especially when they are hearing them from those in authority.

When I was eight years old, I was bullied by my public school principal, Mr. Salmon. I can't forget him. I was sent to his office for using rude language, as reported to my teacher by a fellow student. I had never heard the words I was accused of using. We were admonished at home for saying shut-up! Trust me, to this very day, I do not say "shut-up."

I just remember looking up - way up - he seemed at least 10 feet tall. He had his hands on my shoulders shaking me, telling me that if I didn't admit to the "crime," I would be suspended. At first, I refused to confess something I had not done. But the Principal won. He was bigger than I and far more powerful. That was enough to for me. I pled guilty because I wanted to go home. People will admit to many things when afraid.

I have since learned that Mr. Salmon's bullying could be described as "instrumental" or "coercive" aggression.[1] It is bullying that is purpose-driven, not fear- or anger-driven. It demonstrates an absence of ethics and compassion. It is bullying that has a tangible goal, carried out under intellectual control and will involve only sufficient violence to achieve its goal, influencing social outcomes. Mr. Salmon wanted me to confess, no matter what. And I did. I submitted.

Why am I telling you this story? Because our way of life is under attack by an abusive Industrialized Bullying Machine called the Progressives who are evangelizing a new religion with its own apostles who abhor free speech, free will, and the idea of equality. They are promoting "equity" which inevitably becomes fascism/totalitarianism. George Orwell wrote that almost any English person would accept "bully" as a synonym for

---

1 https://opentextbc.ca/psychologyopenstax/chapter/aggression/.

"Fascist."[2] Disagree and you will be shunned, cut off, shamed, ostracized, canceled, doxed (your personal information shared on social media), silenced and bullied into submission.

> [M]any places in Europe and North America see this resurgence or reinvention of Fascist ideology and organizations as possible causes and consequences of epidemic mental illness (panic, depression, anxiety, and addiction), which become ever more necessary to examine, along with what makes a "sane society."[3]

Fear is being used to bring us in line with the new ideology. That fear affects our children. Too many are under stress and falling into mental illness from the constant industrialized bullying in school, from kindergarten through university, and too many parents are afraid to speak up for them. Fear itself compromises our immune systems and can lead to depression, which renders us incapable of fully responding to real threats. Decisions based on fear often go against our best interests. "Do not fear" is repeated 365 times in the Bible. Once for each day of the year.

Some mental illness is genetic and tends to run in families. If one has a predisposition to mental illness, then illness can be triggered by events in one's life. If we continue to bully our young people, then we will have generations of people unable to cope with the common stress of everyday life. Perhaps that is the purpose of all this bullying by the left: to destroy the individual.

Perhaps we need a new designation for this epidemic of mental illness called "Culturally Acquired Psychosis," a gross break with reality caused not from actual psychosis, a mental disorder, but the result of impaired mental function derived from the culture itself. Rather than a mental disorder primari-

---

2 George Orwell, "As I Please" column in the *London Tribune*, March 24, 1944. Source: http://alexpeak.com/twr/wif/.

3 Emma Dane York, "Disorder: Contemporary Fascism and the Crisis in Mental Health," Graduate thesis University of Saskatchewan, 2018. Source: https://core.ac.uk/download/pdf/226113301.pdf.

ly due to a brain malfunction resulting in atypical information processing, it represents normal brain processing of disinformation that is repeated over and over in schools, mainstream media, and oligarch-controlled social media – being forced to accept as true that which they know to be untrue.

Culturally acquired psychosis is a marvelous expression. It speaks to a type of mass hysteria promoted by fear—fear of being left out or fear of being thrown out. There is also collective obsessional behavior. This is a sociological concept that refers to the phenomenon of masses of people becoming distressed about a perceived—usually unreal or exaggerated—threat portrayed in catastrophizing terms by the media. Think about the fear spread because of the Chinese virus, covid-19.

I suggest all of this is being spread with the assistance of a whole new group of social media experts called "Influencers," today's new heroes. The purpose of an influencer is to change how we behave.

> According to a 2019 survey from Common Sense Media and Survey Monkey, "Teens get their news more frequently from social media sites (e.g., Facebook and Twitter) or from YouTube than directly from news organizations. More than half of teens (54%) get news from social media, and 50% get news from YouTube at least a few times a week. Fewer than half, 41%, get news reported by news organizations in print or online at least a few times a week, and only 37% get news on TV at least a few times a week." Among teens who received their news from YouTube, two-thirds reported learning about the news from celebrities and influencers, rather than news organizations.[4]

So, what is an influencer?

The figure of an influencer is supposed to change how we

---

4   Source: https://www.federalregister.gov/documents/2021/04/19/2021-08068/proposed-priorities-american-history-and-civics-education#print.

behave, to be a spokesperson who should show a deep sense of appreciation (for something), rather than appropriation. It's an influencer's responsibility to create experiences, ideas and ways of thinking that entice crowds to follow them.[5]

Many of these influencers have from hundreds of thousands to millions of followers.

These influencers are speaking to your children in their bedrooms—without you there to mediate—teaching them morals and values that may not be yours but which fit in with today's cancel culture. They are like pedophiles and bullies who surreptitiously come after your children online.

I remember people of influence. They did not have the title Influencer. They didn't need the title. They just influenced by example. They certainly were not given the responsibility to create ways of thinking! What a sense of self-importance we have given to these individuals.

These people may or may not be celebrities. But they have found a voice on social media that calls out to other like-minded people and encourages people to become part of the group or feel left out. There are all types of influencers, from transgender influencers that your children can find online who will tell them that yes, it is wonderful to be transgender, to those who promote Critical Race Theory.

As a very good friend shared with me: "A person with a laptop is more dangerous than a dictator with a missile."

I submit that all of the political bullying taking place today in social media, mainstream media, education and government is a form of instrumental aggression--industrialized bullying--because at the leadership/strategic level, it is done with a specific purposeful gain in mind. It is not done defensively out of a sense of fear, nor out of a sense of anger. It does not run its course until the aggressor reaches a stage of exhaustion. It cannot terminate because the political goal is never completed. Any

---

5 Chidozie Obasi, "What role can and should influencers play in the BLM movement?" *Harper's Bazaar*, June 23, 2020.

level of violence necessary to achieve its end is justified as "fair." That violence is not just physical. It is violence done to the soul, to the very essence of life.

To understand the damage being done to our way of life, we need to be familiar with Critical Race Theory, wokeness, cancel culture and most importantly, Western Culture and the ethic that underpins freedom, for it is our culture that is under attack from these malicious ideologies and our children who will suffer the most.

2
The Silencing of America

Much of the country believes that America is racist, cruel, and incapable of self-correction of its so-called original sins — without a radical erasure of much of its past history, traditions, and customs. – Victor Davis Hanson[1]

S OMETHING HAS GONE AWRY in America, once home of the brave, land of the free where one could pursue happiness relatively unmolested. Today, America is being bullied into submission by an ideology that promotes self-centered tribalism rather than the grand experiment of a multiethnic society that is the West and in particular America. Life and liberty are under attack from within. A massive paradigm shift is taking place. Freedom and free will are under attack from a left-wing progressive ideology that includes the woke preaching of true believers in Black Lives Matter and Critical Race Theory with their rants about white privilege, the demonization of men and the repudiation of the nuclear family. These are direct attacks on the very foundation of the country, the Judeo-Christian ethic which promotes freedom, free speech, and free will, the ethic which underpins the American Constitution.

Remember when President Barack Obama derided people

---

1   Victor Davis Hanson, "2020 Election Will Be a Contest of the Angry," *National Review Online*, June 25, 2020.

23

who hold on to their guns and religion?

> You go into these small towns in Pennsylvania and, like a lot of small towns in the Midwest, the jobs have been gone now for 25 years and nothing's replaced them... They get bitter; they cling to guns or religion...[2]

Religion?

This was a direct salvo against the very ethic that is meant to tie Americans together.

This religious ethic that underpins the American Constitution states that all people are born with equal intrinsic value (all are equal before God) and all life is sacred. This is taken to mean we mustn't judge people based on superficial characteristics, such as race, colour, creed, religion or sexual orientation, but rather by their characters. The ethic that came out of the Judean desert 3500 years ago taught us that we are the subjects of our destiny, not the objects of our fate. We are neither born into the manor nor are we born to be subservient. We have what Jason D. Hill, professor of philosophy and Honors Distinguished Faculty at DePaul University in Chicago, calls moral agency: free will. And that same ethic promotes freedom of thought and of speech. It was the prophet Jeremiah who died defending free speech.

Moral agency has been very important to Professor Hill. In his book *We Have Overcome*, he explains that he has fought against victimhood/victimology for a long time. We choose to be active participants in our lives or we choose to be victims. He writes of the danger of tribal collectivism and groupthink and the danger of herd and horde mentality. He has fought against the philosophical credo regarding blacks in America: that black people cannot do well in a "white America," that they have no moral agency. However, he writes, "left-wingers heed the call of black dependence with glee because it places them in a perma-

---

2 See Ben Smith, "Obama on small-town Pa.: Clinging to religion, guns, xenophobia," *Politico*, April 11, 2008.

nent position of power..."[3]

Professor Hill is a black, gay man born in Jamaica. At the age of ten, he knew that America was the light unto the nations for him, and in America, he could be whomever he chose. At twenty, he arrived in America and he succeeded, albeit not without pain and suffering. He admires America, which sadly far too many don't, because as he wrote, one has "the inviolable freedom to create one's own conception of the good life for oneself."[4]

Progressives are attempting to destroy America by attacking America at its roots: first by denying her origins as a nation with a constitution in 1776 by stating that America began in 1619. No it didn't. The North American continent was filled with British, French, English, Dutch, and Spanish colonies at that time. The Progressives are also censoring all who do not fall into line with their left-wing ideology, aided and abetted by accusations of white oppression, diversity (divisiveness to divide and conquer), identity politics which dehumanize individuals by taking away their individual identities and lumping them into groups, and Critical Race Theory, all supported by the Democratic Party and all contrary to America's foundational ethic.

It is unethical to lump people into groups: both unethical and immoral. From the early 1900s, psychologists have known that individuals differ considerably not only in intelligence but also in temperament and personality factors. Decisions concerning individuals should be made on the basis of the specific individual and not on the basis of his or her group characteristics. Identity politics, which judges individuals solely on alleged group characteristics, is consequently generally wrong and always unethical.

The Progressive Left is targeting politicians, journalists, professors, businesses, and parents who refuse to bend the knee to their new ideology by threatening cancelation, that is, ban-

---

3   Jason D. Hill, *We Have Overcome: An Immigrant's Letter to the American People*, Bombardier Books, 2020, p. 101.

4   Ibid., p. 59.

ishment from polite society and possibly much worse, including loss of livelihood.

This new ideology does not include reverence for God, which used to orient society under a just and merciful transcendence.

In 2011, a young man named Tim Tebow, , the quarterback for the Denver Broncos, took a knee and bowed his head during a football game.[5] He took a lot of flak for his faith. "Players from other teams, as well as fans, have openly mocked and ridiculed Tebow's Christian beliefs, and even media outlets have taken jabs at his faith, albeit in mostly subtle ways. Still, Tebow remained steadfast and attracted the attention of fellow Christian Kurt Warner, a former quarterback for the New York Giants and St. Louis Rams, who had some advice for Tebow: *Tone down the public displays of your faith*."[6] Why? Why should the response be to tone down one's beliefs - but only when one believes in God? How is this small display of faith detrimental to the public?

Then in 2017, we witnessed Colin Kaepernick taking a knee during the American National Anthem. Not after a touchdown, during the National Anthem. And he was praised by the media and the left. He was never advised to tone down his beliefs.

Kaepernick is a young man blessed to be adopted in a loving family. A white family. Able to reach his dreams with their help and the help of others. What a gift he received. So many others with similar ability just didn't get that brass ring. But he did. He could have shared his gratitude everywhere. He had two choices in life as do each and every one of us. He could look at this moment—a snapshot—and choose to be bitter, or choose to be better. Kaepernick chose bitter. And he spread that bitterness everywhere. Look how easy it was for so many others, as blessed as he, to jump on the bitterness wagon in spite of their

---

5 Raven Clabough, "Christian NFL Player Tim Tebow Takes Heat for His Faith." *New American*, December 2, 2011.

6 Brendan Giusti, "Tim Tebow Subjected to Faith-Based Taunts for Second Week Running," *The Christian Post*, November 6, 2011.

multimillion-dollar NFL salaries.

During the Tokyo Olympics that took place the summer of 2021, all but one of the US women's soccer team players knelt before the Olympic bronze-medal match. Carli Lloyd stood as her teammates took a knee before kickoff — after the national anthem played, to protest racism and discrimination.[7]

The most egregious attack on America's Constitution are the calls by black people for white people to kneel before them begging for forgiveness. "Please pardon us, grant us atonement for the crime of being white." Nothing is more dangerous. This call to kneel, and the response, is vile, divisive, malevolent and vengeful. These are attacks on the very soul of America.

The Progressives will not be happy with their calls for "diversity, inclusion, equity" (DIE) and their attacks on "white privilege." Oh no. They want to take down the "republic for which it [the flag] stands."

---

7 Meredith Cash, "All but one of the US women's soccer starters knelt to protest racism ahead of the team's Olympic bronze-medal match," *Insider*, April 5, 2021.

3
Critical Thinking[1]

Every part of thinking should be questioned, doubted, and tested. —René Descartes

Democracy cannot succeed unless those who express their choice are prepared to choose wisely. The real safeguard of democracy, therefore, is education. —Franklin D. Roosevelt

HERE WAS A TIME when we were taught the importance of critical thinking and objective truth: truth based on facts, not feelings. Critical thinking was a bulwark against bullying, especially the bullying by the Progressive Left. We cannot have a discussion about Progressive ideology and its effects without first talking about critical thinking—something that is no longer taught to our children in school.

There was a time, not so long ago, when one was encouraged to ask questions! Schoolchildren were taught logic and reasoning skills and were encouraged to study opposing views and to study related fields in both the sciences and philosophy, including the philosophy of religion. A child was encouraged to find reasons for his beliefs that would not only satisfy himself

---

1 This chapter is also contained in my previous book, *The #IslamophobiaIndustry: The Insidious Infiltration of Islam into the West*, Independently published, 2021.

28

but would be persuasive to others. He was taught to seek the truth, whatever it may be and wherever it may be found, regardless of what one might wish to be true.

As philosopher Martin Heidegger wrote, "[Q]uestioning is the piety of thought."[2] We should seek not only to criticize but to understand other viewpoints and to humbly acknowledge when we are wrong.

> Deep questions drive our thoughts underneath the surface of things and force us to deal with complexity. Questions of purpose force us to define our task. Questions of information force us to look at our sources of information as well as at the quality of our information. Questions of interpretation force us to examine how we are organizing or giving meaning to information and to consider alternative ways of giving meaning. Questions of assumption force us to examine what we are taking for granted. Questions of implication force us to follow out where our thinking is going. Questions of point of view force us to examine our point of view and to consider other relevant points of view. Questions of relevance force us to discriminate what does and what does not bear on a question. Questions of accuracy force us to evaluate and test for truth and correctness. Questions of precision force us to give details and be specific. Questions of consistency force us to examine our thinking for contradictions. Questions of logic force us to consider how we are putting the whole of our thought together, to make sure that it all adds up and makes sense within a reasonable system of some kind.
>
> The goal of critical thinking is to establish a disciplined "executive" level of thinking to our thinking, a powerful inner voice of reason, to monitor, assess, and re-constitute — in a more rational direction — our thinking, feeling, and action. Socratic discussion cultivates that inner voice by providing a public model for it.[3]

---

2 Martin Heidegger, *The Question Concerning Technology*, p. 41. https:// philtech.michaelreno.org/wp-content/uploads/2020/05/HeideggerTheQuestionConcerningTechnology.pdf.

3 "The Role of Socratic Questioning in Thinking, Teaching, and Learning,"

The intellectual roots of critical thinking are ultimately traceable to Socrates, undoubtedly the greatest educator the world has ever known, who taught by asking questions which elicited answers from his students (the Socratic method).

> Twenty-five hundred years ago he discovered by a method of probing questioning that people could not rationally justify their confident claims to knowledge... He established the importance of asking deep questions that probe profoundly into thinking before we accept ideas as worthy of belief... In the Renaissance (15th and 16th Centuries), a flood of scholars in Europe began to think critically about religion, art, society, human nature, law, and freedom. They proceeded with the assumption that most of the domains of human life were in need of searching analysis and critique. Among these scholars were Colet, Erasmus, and Moore in England. They followed up on the insight of the ancients... Francis Bacon, in England, was explicitly concerned with the way we misuse our minds in seeking knowledge: "Idols of the market-place" (the ways we misuse words), Descartes wrote: "Every part of thinking should be questioned, doubted, and tested."

> The critical thinking of these Renaissance and post-Renaissance scholars opened the way for the emergence of science and for the development of democracy, human rights, and freedom for thought... Locke defended a common sense analysis of everyday life and thought. He laid the theoretical foundation for critical thinking about basic human rights and the responsibilities of all governments to submit to the reasoned criticism of thoughtful citizens... William Graham Sumner 1906 wrote "Criticism is the examination and test of propositions of any kind which are offered for acceptance, in order to find out whether they correspond to reality or not.' Ludwig Wittgenstein; 'We have increased our awareness not only of the importance of concepts in human thought, but also of the need to analyze concepts and assess their power and

---

The Foundation for Critical Thinking, https://www.criticalthinking.org/pages/the-role-of-socratic-questioning-in-thinking-teaching-amp-learning/522.

limitations."[4]

> [I]t is questions that fuel political discussion and debate, and determine, to a large extent, what is available for comment and analysis, and what is left unsaid. Questions play a vital, and often unnoticed, role in the political landscape... By asking a question, a person asserts their right to be a part of the discussion and to have their concerns taken into account... Secondly, asking questions is a familiar and effective way of getting information. This is, once again, a simple but powerful function of questions: it could indeed be viewed as their primary function. When we ask questions we are often, perhaps typically, trying to find things out. In doing so, we gather information about topics and issues that interest or concern us, whether it be out of pure curiosity, or for practical or political reasons.[5]

Michael Scriven and Richard Paul attempted to define critical thinking:

> Critical thinking is the intellectually disciplined process of actively and skillfully conceptualizing, applying, analyzing, synthesizing, and/or evaluating information gathered from, or generated by, observation, experience, reflection, reasoning, or communication, as a guide to belief and action. In its exemplary form, it is based on universal intellectual values that transcend subject matter divisions: clarity, accuracy, precision, consistency, relevance, sound evidence, good reasons, depth, breadth, and fairness.[6]

---

4   Richard Paul, Linda Elder, and Ted Bartell, "A Brief History of the Idea of Critical Thinking," in *The Foundation for Critical Thinking*, taken from the *California Teacher Preparation for Instruction in Critical Thinking: Research Findings and Policy Recommendations: State of California, California Commission on Teacher Credentialing*, Sacramento, CA, March 1997.

5   Lani Watson, "Good Democracy Needs Good Questions," Cardiff blog, *Open for Debate*, September 25, 2017.

6   Michael Scriven and Richard Paul, "Defining Critical Thinking," *Foundation for Critical Thinking*. http://www.criticalthinking.org/pages/defining-critical-thinking/766.

Greg Lukianoff and Jonathan Haidt, in their article and subsequent book, *The Coddling of the American Mind*, write that "critical thinking encourages students to question their own unexamined beliefs, as well as the received wisdom of those around them."[7]

Questions facilitate informed decision-making. Yet, here we are silencing questions from those who see the world through a different light or lens. Progressivism is demanding that we give up our individual opinions and accept their world view as gospel, that we not only silence these questions in ourselves, but turn to attack those who ask them with a "vindictive protectiveness" which creates "a culture in which everyone must think twice before speaking up, lest they face charges of insensitivity, aggression, or worse."[8]

Refusing to parrot progressive ideology very often leads to complete banishment from the public square—an intolerable situation for any thinking person.

7 Greg Lukianoff and Jonathan Haidt, "The Coddling of the American Mind," *The Atlantic*, September 2015.

8 Ibid.

4
What is Western Culture?

May the same wonder-working Deity, who long since deliv-
ered the Hebrews from their Egyptian oppressors, planted them
in a promised land—whose providential agency has lately been
conspicuous in establishing these United States as an independent
nation—still continue to water them with the dews of heaven and
make the inhabitants of every denomination participate in the
temporal and spiritual blessings of that people whose God is Je-
hovah.
—George Washington
Letter to Congregation Mickve Israel in Georgia, 1789.

WESTERN CULTURE HAS roots in the distant Hebraic and Hellenic past. In 2015, I wrote *Back to the Ethic: Reclaiming Western Values[1]* to help explain the origin of our freedoms in the teachings of the Hebrew Bible. This is an ideology that demands we honour life because ALL life is the gift of God and therefore sacred. It follows that all people are born with equal intrinsic value—a worthy ideal.

In addition, we have free will or moral agency that demands of us that we choose, and choose wisely from the ethics it bequeaths to us. It is an ethic, a culture that honours the ma-

---

1 See Diane Bederman, *Back to the Ethic: Reclaiming Western Values,* Mantua Books, 2015.

jority while protecting the individual and hence the minority.

> In every genuine democracy today, majority rule is both endorsed and limited by the supreme law of the constitution, which protects the rights of individuals. Tyranny by minority over the majority is barred, but so is tyranny of the majority against minorities.[2]

This ethic also broke with the ancient understanding of time which was considered circular, with no beginning and no end—living life like a hamster in a wheel, one's contributions unimportant to the future. The Bible, instead, teaches us that time is linear. That means that each of us matters. Our actions affect the future and so we learn from the past in order to improve the prospects for the future, and thus, may bring about a just way of life. History and culture are therefore cumulative. Sigmund Freud commented on culture as follows:

> [T]he sum of the achievements and institutions which differentiate our lives from those of our animal forbears and served two purposes namely that of protecting humanity against nature and of regulating the relations of humans among themselves.[3]

In his 1927 edition of *The History of Philosophy*, Will Durant noted the concept of "wedded history:"

> History can become philosophy only by being not analytic but synthetic: not shredded history, but wedded history, history in which all phases of life in a given period shall be studied in their correlation in their common response to similar conditions …That would be the picture of an age…[4]

---

2 Annenberg Classroom, *Majority Rule Minority Rights.* https://www.annenbergclassroom.org/glossary_term/majority-rule-and-minority-rights/.

3 Sigmund Freud, *Civilization and its Discontents*, Penguin, 2002, first published in English, 1930, pp. 49-50.

4 Will Durant, *The History of Philosophy*, Simon and Schuster, 1927, pp. 516-17.

The Judeo-Christian ethic contains the ideal to which we should aspire. It is the ethic that urges us to look at the past and say the following:

> [W]hile America's founders were guilty of undeniable hypocrisy, their own moral failings did not invalidate their transformational project. The founding documents were not evil to the core but "magnificent," as Martin Luther King Jr. put it, because they were "a promissory note to which every American was to fall heir." In other words: The founders themselves planted the seeds of slavery's destruction. And our second founding fathers—abolitionists like Frederick Douglass—made it so. America would never be perfect, but we could always strive toward building a more perfect union.[5]

Creating a better society in the New World was the religious mission of the Pilgrims who had suffered oppression in the Old World.

> The founders of America sought religious freedom because of European religious intolerance. They favored economic freedom because they suffered under the English monopoly, mercantile system. The desire for social freedom comes in part from rejection of the English class system. The expansiveness of the country is itself a geography of freedom.

> Just as freedom is the American dream in so many areas of life, freedom is extremely important for good mental health. Good mental health is characterized by having personal freedom – to be free to make good choices for one's self and others.[6]

According to historical documents, the Puritans who first

---

5 Bari Weiss, "Stop Being Shocked," *Tablet*, October 14, 2020.
6 Don Carroll, "Freedom and Mental Health," *North Carolina Lawyers Assistance Program*, April 8, 2014. https://www.nclap.org/freedom-mental-health/.

arrived on America's shores brought the Hebrew Bible with them, sharing the words of the prophets, lawgivers, and sages of Israel. Indeed, the Bible provided the framework for the newly established democracy.

> Universities including Harvard, Yale, Columbia (formerly King's College) University of Chicago, and William and Mary taught Hebrew Scripture; the morals and values it contained that would underpin all documents. The colonists believed in the need for the imposition of an outside code of laws.
>
> (...)
>
> In them, the colonists felt, was to be found democracy as they understood it.
>
> (...)
>
> The Mosaic rulings...were used as a supreme authority when any occasion arose that required the citation of a precedent.[7]

America's early leaders such as George Washington and John Adams were steeped in the teaching of the Jewish people. John Adams, a member of the Declaration of Independence committee and second president of the United States (1797–1801), understood the deep connection between ethical monotheism and freedom:

> I will insist that the Hebrews have done more to civilize men than any other nation. If I were an atheist, and believed in blind eternal fate, I should still believe that fate had ordained the Jews to be the most essential instrument for civilizing the nations. If I were an atheist of the other sect, who believe or pretend to believe that all is ordered by chance, I should believe that chance had ordered the Jews to preserve and propagate to all mankind the doctrine of a supreme, intelligent, wise, almighty, sovereign of the universe, which I believe to be a great essential prin-

---

7 Dagobert D. Runes, *The Hebrew Impact on Western Civilization*, Philosophical Library, New York, 1951.

ciple of all morality, and consequently of all civilization.[8]

8 John Adams, Letter to François Adriaan van der Kemp (February 16, 1809). Source: https://quotepark.com/quotes/1924395-john-adams-i-will-insist-that-the-hebrews-have-done-more-to-c/.

5

Malignant Morality and Normality

THE WORLD WATCHED as Germany morphed from being a country renowned for its Enlightenment contributions, giving the world great thinkers such as Leibniz, Kant, and Goethe, into one taken over and thoroughly degraded by Adolph Hitler. Citizens of all classes followed the orders of Hitler, snitching on neighbours, turning in Jews to be taken away and murdered, as well as standing by while mentally and physically disabled people were exterminated. How was this possible?

The answer may be malignant normality: the way average people—most of us—drift or slide or shuffle or stumble into moral corruption. Psychiatrist Robert Jay Lifton, most famous as the author of *The Nazi Doctors: Medical Killing and the Psychology of Genocide,* suggests we are socialized into "malignant normality." Evil ideologies shape our thinking even when we think we're resisting them. According to Lifton, Hitler preached "a genocidal ideology." It offered:

> a biomedical vision as a kind of explanation of history: namely, that the Nordic race had once been healthy and dominant as the only culture-creating race; that it became "infected" by destructive Jewish influence and rendered weak and ill; and that it could become healthy and strong again only by ridding it of that Jewish influence.

[...]

Extreme ideologues do much to create a malignant normality, which comes to pervade most institutions, including medical ones.[1]

David Mills, former editor of *First Things,* continues:

> Because social elites and so many of his peers believe the same thing, he does not see how warped the vision of things has become. He accepts the malignant normality as normality. It's the way things are. Everyone knows that. So he thinks.[2]

Dr. John Gartner, a practicing psychotherapist who taught at Johns Hopkins University Medical School, explains malignant normality:

> Malignant normality is when a malignantly narcissistic leader takes control of a society and gradually changes reality for everyone else.[3]

Bandy X Lee, who "diagnosed" Donald Trump from afar, is also concerned about malignant normality.[4]

These authors, and others, labeled Donald Trump as the narcissistic leader of malignant normality. A Hitler. Donald Trump was the President who brought about the Abraham Accords, sanctions on Iran and China, closed the southern border to illegal aliens, made America energy independent, and brought hope back to Middle America.

I agree that a malignant normality is taking place in America, but not from a narcissistic leader—rather from a Progres-

---

1 Source: David Mills' review of *The Nazi Doctors: Medical Killing and the Psychology of Genocide* by Robert Jay Lifton in *The Human Life Review,* June 2017. https://humanlifereview.com/malignant-normality/.

2 Ibid.

3 Source: Michael Payne, "Malignant normality silently takes hold in America," *Nation of Change,* December 5, 2019. https://www.nationofchange.org/2019/12/05/malignant-normality-silently-takes-hold-in-america/.

4 Bandy X. Lee M.D., "Mental Health Experts Warn of a Malignant Normality," *Psychology Today,* May 29, 2018.

sive left-wing ideology that is infiltrating every level of American society, from education to media to government, changing the mores of society. Malignant normality thrives by silencing opposition and promoting submission to the new value system. These ideas negate the Judeo-Christian ethic that underpins freedom in the West. Now this Progressive value system is running rampant throughout the culture.

Whoever thought it possible that one day a theology professor, Chanequa Walker-Barnes, would write a prayer to God to help her to hate white people?

> I want to stop caring about them (white people), individually and collectively. I want to stop caring about their misguided, racist souls, to stop believing that they can be better, that they can stop being racist.[5]

This is possible because the left is implementing industrialized bullying, shaming, shunning, canceling, and silencing anyone who does not agree with their views on Critical Race Theory, white privilege, or their new definition of the family. The past is viewed as an inferior state of existence which cannot be learned from but must instead be erased in order to purge its malign influence on the present. Just as Hitler preached his view of history, the Progressives are doing the same thing—obliterating the past, and the lessons we were to have learned, while rewriting history in their own image.

When we betray our own moral sense and commit some transgression against another or ourselves, we eventually become conscious of the transgression, and guilt or shame result. It is no secret that many Germans felt shame after the Nazi years. How could their parents and grandparents have participated in any way, including as a bystander?

What will happen here in the next few generations if Progressive left-wing ideologies take over and transform America?

---

5 Chanequa Walker-Barnes, "Prayer of a Weary Black Woman" in *A Rhythm of Prayer: A Collection of Meditations for Renewal.* Source: https://www.breitbart.com/tech/2021/04/17/mercer-u-theology-profs-prayer-dear-god-please-help-me-to-hate-white-people/.

Their ideology is diametrically opposed to the Constitution and the moral and ethical values upon which it stands—free-will (moral agency), free speech and freedom for all based on character, not characteristics. If people do not stand up to this bullying, will the next generation suffer from shame when they learn that their parents got on their knees and asked forgiveness for being white? Will they suffer from shame because their parents gave in to Critical Race Theory and white privilege? Will people of colour suffer from shame because their parents and grandparents gave in to victimhood?

As Thomas Jefferson said, "Eternal vigilance is the price of freedom." Writing in the voice of his father, Albin, who was a soldier in the German Army during the Second World War, Douglas Gagel maintains:

> [W]arfare is an excuse for taking away personal freedoms, for enslaving a nation's own citizens. Warfare dehumanizes people, removing their individual identities, and enables persons in power to treat people like objects to be used and disposed of without punitive consequences for those in charge.

> Hardest to understand may be that a nations' own leaders can be the people's worst enemy. Beware when your government proposes to take away civil rights in order to protect people from "enemies of the nation," no matter who those enemies are purported to be. Be suspicious of patriotism as it is a convenient tool of tyranny. Do not be fooled by the media's support for militaristic actions, no matter how righteous it sounds; rather weigh the costs with common sense, question the motives of those who stand to gain from these actions, and listen to your conscience. Remember your responsibility to keep political leaders honest, to guard against your government eroding personal rights and freedoms, and resist any and all self-serving clamour for war. Exercising that responsibility can involve personal effort, risk and even hardship, but history has repeatedly demonstrated that the consequenc-

es of doing nothing are far worse.[6]

The Progressive left is promoting a malignant new morality of victimhood that if implemented would destroy America.

How are they managing to do this? By pitting two groups against each other: people of colour (the oppressed victims) against people of no color (the oppressor victimizers). Divide and conquer. If successful, this malignant substitute for morality, based on equity and victimology will, like cancer, spread over time. It will destroy the Judeo-Christian ethic which states that all people are born with equal intrinsic value—the foundation of all of America's freedoms. It will leave Americans in a state of malignant normality achieved with lies and psychological coercion from constant bullying in the name of diversity, inclusion and equity. (DIE) And too many among us are doing nothing.

Empires have risen and fallen over the millennia for many reasons. The Roman Empire had a strong political government and maintained economic prosperity for several centuries; and yet, it fell. The British Empire likewise collapsed. War depleted her treasury. The Ottoman Empire is gone. The capital of the Eastern Roman Empire, Constantinople, was conquered by the Ottoman army under the command of Ottoman Sultan Mehmed II on 29 May 1453. With this conquest, the Ottomans became an empire and one of the most powerful empires. Then, World War I ended that empire as well.

Today, one might classify the West as an Empire of democratic countries firmly rooted in the Judeo-Christian ethic that underpins all of their constitutions. This ethic requires discipline—the ability to repress and suppress one's instincts, particularly those that relate to vengeance and sex. It requires giving up some freedoms for the sake of community. This creates a living social contract as described by philosophers Thomas Hobbes, John Locke, and Jean-Jacques Rousseau. The social

---

6　Douglas Wolfgang Oskar Gagel, *Fuhrer, Folk and Fatherland* written in the voice of his father Albin Gagel, a soldier in the German Army in the Second World War. Albin moved his family to Canada. Self-published, 2016. https://www.amazon.ca/Fuhrer-Folk-Fatherland-Soldiers-Story/dp/0995209103.

contract is an agreement that makes it possible for citizens to "give up certain of their rights and freedoms, handing them over to a central authority, which in return, will ensure the rule of law within the society and the defense of the realm against external enemies."[7]

The Empire will be destroyed if the King is killed. The King is the ethic.

We are being lulled, whether by apathy or ignorance, into accepting ideologies and values that conflict with Western Culture. The latest attack began in the 1960s. At that time, FBI Director J. Edgar Hoover called attention to radical professors who were propagandizing, organizing, and operationalizing college students for political purposes. But it seems we did nothing. Because of our silence, we are faced with greater threats today. Our intentions have been good, but good intentions have been known to pave the road to perdition. Unintended consequences are catching up to us. Western culture is clearly in decline, but there is still time to prevent the fall.

The greatest threat to freedom is coming from within American culture itself. If it is not stopped, America, the best of the West, will implode. America is being bullied into submission from within. Left-wing ideologies are colonizing America, taking us away from our values that teach we are subjects of our destiny and not the objects of fate. We are not born into our "place" in a caste system from which there is no escape, although this is essentially what is being taught in our schools. We are not to be judged by our immutable characteristics—skin color, race, gender—over which we have no control. Well, until today, when we are told that despite the fact that we are born male or female, we can change our sex at will.

Our ethic teaches us that we are to be judged by character. The new "ethic" preaches that racism in America is systemic and we must relearn history through the lens of Critical Race Theory and white privilege which defines us by our characteris-

---

7   Rabbi Jonathan Sacks, Ebor Lectures 2011, presented at St. John University, York, England, November 30, 2011. http://www.rabbisacks.org/biblical-insights-into-the-good-society-ebor-lecture-2012/.

tics. And if we do not obey—kneel to the new ethic—then we will be silenced and bullied into submission.

These ideologues know that coercion will succeed when persuasion fails. And yet, many bullies will back down at the first sign of resistance. Resist![8]

I can't imagine what Martin Luther King Jr would say today, when not too long ago, he wrote: "I have a dream that my four children will one day live in a nation where they will not be judged by the colour of their skin, but by the content of their character."[9]

Winston Churchill, who knew all too well about democracy and Western culture, wrote: "Many forms of Government have been tried, and will be tried in this world of sin and woe. No one pretends that democracy is perfect or all-wise. Indeed, it has been said that democracy is the worst form of Government except all those others that have been tried from time to time."[10]

Plato warned us: "Dictatorship naturally arises out of democracy, and the most aggravated form of tyranny and slavery out of the most extreme liberty."[11]

Extreme tolerance, inclusion and accommodation can be linked to extreme liberty: accepting that which is incompatible in the name of freedom leads to tolerating the intolerable.

This is suicide by democracy.

---

8 See Patrick Allan, "How to Handle Being Bullied as an Adult," *Lifehacker*, December 1, 2020.

9 Martin Luther King Jr., "I Have a Dream" speech delivered August 28, 1963.

10 Winston S Churchill, November 11, 1947.

11 Plato, *The Republic*.

6

Progressivism: the 21st Century's New Religion of The Woke

We are not content with negative obedience, nor even with the most abject submission. When finally you surrender to us, it must be of your own free will. —George Orwell, *1984*

W E MUST WAKE UP before the woke take over.
Woke: a state of being aware, especially of social problems such as racism and inequality. It means being conscious of racial discrimination in society and other forms of oppression and injustice. In mainstream use, woke can also describe someone or something as being "with it." Steve Rose explained the origins of woke:

> The origins of woke, in this context – as forged by African American communities – dates back at least to the 60s, but its mainstream ubiquity is a recent development. Fuelled by black musicians, social media and the #BlackLives-Matter movement, the term entered the Oxford English Dictionary only in 2017, by which time it had become as much a fashionable buzzword as a set of values. Some of those who didn't keep up with the trend felt left behind: if you didn't know the meaning of woke, you weren't.

Rather than rejecting the concept of wokeness outright,

today's detractors often claim they are rejecting the word
as a signifier of pretentiousness and "cultural elitism".
However (...) it is as much to do with the issues of racial
and social justice. Criticizing "woke culture" has become
a way of claiming victim status for yourself rather than ac-
knowledging that more deserving others hold that status.[1]

Think about that. It is a fight for the right to be the number one victim. Today, "woke" means to identify as a staunch
social justice advocate who is abreast of contemporary political
concerns — or to be perceived that way. As explained by Aja
Romano:

[I]n 2014, following the police killing of Michael Brown
in Ferguson, Missouri, "stay woke" suddenly became the
cautionary watchword of Black Lives Matter activists on
the streets, used in a chilling and specific context: keeping
watch for police brutality and unjust police tactics.
(...)
[S]ince Brown's death, "woke" has evolved into a sin-
gle-word summation of leftist political ideology, centered
on social justice politics and critical race theory.
(...)
Ferguson was true social awakening for many activists and progressives — and as part of this moment, the
idea of staying aware of or "woke" to the inequities of
the American justice system was a heady one. While the
#BlackLivesMatter hashtag served as a locus of informa-
tion and organization during the Ferguson protests, the
#StayWoke hashtag arguably served an equally important
emotional and spiritual purpose: It allowed Black citizens
to unite around a shared perception [I suggest, of vic-
timization] and experience of reality — and to galvanize
themselves and each other for a very long fight for change.
(...)
Historian and Christian theorist Jemar Tisby said he
found the idea of a religious awakening to be powerful
— even as he noted that "woke," like so many appropriat-

---

1 Steve Rose, "How the word 'woke' was weaponised by the right," *The
Guardian*, January 21, 2020.

ed Black words and ideas, had "hit the mainstream" and then [been] voided of some of its meaning and potency in the process "If you really delve into the metaphor of being woke," he said, "it implies that in some sense you were asleep to particular kinds of injustices and oppressions in the world, and now you've been awakened to it."[2]

As explained by Diyora Shadijanova:

> Wokeness is generally accepted as the idea that you've woken up to the social injustices around you, seen how oppression has been institutionalized and now are unable to un-see this truth. Essentially, once you're woke, you can't fall asleep.[3]

Woke, a word that came about to protect minorities, now symbolizes a threat to free speech, a way to ruin lives. In practise, it means hating everyone who disagrees with you and having no qualms about bullying them into submission or silence. Victor Davis Hanson writes:

> "Wokeness" is the new religion, growing faster and larger than Christianity. Its priesthood outnumbers the clergy and exercises far more power. Silicon Valley is the new Vatican, and Amazon, Apple, Facebook, Google, and Twitter are the new gospels.[4]

Caroline Downey reveals:

> Google has launched an antiracism program for employees, featuring training workshops and speaker sessions, that teaches the principles of critical race theory, chiefly that America was founded on white supremacy.
> (...)

---

2 Aja Romano, "A history of 'wokeness," *Vox*, October 9, 2020.

3 Diyora Shadijanova, "How did the word 'woke' become weaponised?" *Stylist,* 2022.

4 Victor Davis Hanson, "The 10 Radical New Rules That Are Changing America," *The Epoch Times*, March 31, 2021.

A number of videos presented to employees conveyed the message that racism is an irredeemable stain on America's national fabric and that white people have profited from white supremacy, even if they are innocent of engaging in it personally.[5]

Wokeness includes banning Aunt Jemima, Dr. Seuss, Harry Potter, Mr. Potato Head, Winston Churchill and many others. Everything just Gone…With the Wind.

There is a wonderful book by Dr. Seuss that teaches children about being bullied into submission. Shhhh. I know some of his work has been canceled—racist, don't you know,—but I think this story must be shared.

It is called *Yertle the Turtle*. A happy turtle, king of his pond. The ruler of all he could see. But one day, Yertle decided he wanted more. So he needed to make a bigger throne that would allow him to see more and be king of more. To do that he needed his turtle subjects to stand one upon another, higher and higher. And he bullied them into following his orders. The pain of it all, especially on the turtle at the very bottom, who one day had the courage to complain.

> "Beg your pardon, King Yertle.
> I've pains in my back and my shoulders and knees.
> How long must we stand here, Your Majesty, please?"

> "SILENCE!" the King of the Turtles barked back.
> But that did not stop the turtle named Mack
> "Your Majesty, please… I don't like to complain,
> But down here below, we are feeling great pain.
> I know, up on top you are seeing great sights,
> But down here at the bottom we, too, should have rights.
> We turtles can't stand it. Our shells will all crack!
> Besides, we need food. We are starving!" groaned Mack.

> And then Mack burped, and the throne collapsed.

---

5 Caroline Downey, "Google Launches Antiracism Program Teaching That America Is a 'System of White Supremacy'," *National Review*, September 8, 2021.

And to say the great Yertle, that Marvelous he,
Is King of the Mud. That is all he can see.
And the turtles, of course... all the turtles are free
As turtles and, maybe, all creatures should be.

And all the turtles stood on equal ground, again.[6]

Why am I sharing this story? To teach about being bullied into silence and submission—precursors to fascism—and that bullying is taking place in our schools, against our children. We must overthrow this pernicious ideology with critical thinking and the removal of progressive left-wing ideology that comes from Black Lives Matter, Critical Race Theory, "wokeness," and the rantings about white privilege. These attacks on our culture are an attack on our citizens and their mental health. If we are to keep our freedom, freedom given to us by the 3500-year-old Judeo-Christian ethic, we must succeed.

6 Dr. Seuss, *Yertle the Turtle and Other Stories*, Random House Books for Young Readers, 1958.

7

Cancel Culture

Maybe the ultimate threat to the West comes...from our own lack of understanding of and faith in our own cultural heritage.
—Niall Ferguson, *Civilization: The West and the Rest*

ALLAN BLOOM, author of *The Closing of the American Mind*, 1987, wrote that many of us find our purpose and our intellectual and spiritual connection to the world through the stories and wisdom of the Bible. However, Bloom observed, many of his young students live with "an open-ended future and the lack of a binding past" and are in "a condition like that of the first men in the state of nature spiritually unclad, unconnected, isolated, with no inherited or unconditional connection with anything or anyone."[1]

The West is at war. A battle amongst cultures. I believe this war is only possible because we stopped teaching the Judeo-Christian ethic that underpins freedom. We are leaving our young people at sea.

Western culture promotes freedom, free will, free speech, and the knowledge that one is the subject of one's destiny because one has the right and the obligation to choose his or her own path. This new culture, Cancel Culture, what writer Wesley

---

1 Allan Bloom, *The Closing of the American Mind,* Simon & Schuster, 1987, p. 87.

Yang at the Manhattan Institute refers to as "the successor ideology,"[2] is a culture that takes us back to a time of an artificially designed hierarchy which promotes the belief that one is the object of one's fate, hampered, held back by race, colour, creed, religion or sexual orientation. Failure to adhere to this new ideology can lead to social ostracism or "canceling."

Bari Weiss, former contributor to the *New York Times,* described cancel culture as "social murder." Senator Tom Cotton of Arkansas wrote: "Cancel culture, whether in its Maoist or its Jacobin forms, ultimately is animated by a single idea—that America at its core is fundamentally irredeemable and wicked."[3]

President Donald Trump stated cancel culture was being used as a "political weapon," adding, "It is completely alien to our culture and our values, and it has absolutely no place in the United States of America."[4]

Even President Obama had words to say about the cancel culture trend: "That's not activism. That's not bringing about change. If all you're doing is casting stones, you're probably not going to get that far. That's easy to do."[5]

Cancel culture promotes standing on the shoulders of giants, not to rise up and reach for the stars but to bury those giants in the dust and then blame others for their personal failures. Cancel culture is set on removing all traces of positivity from the West so only a sadly miscontextualized and inaccurate record of Western villainy remains, creating a societal vacuum for the pernicious, misanthropic and cynical woke mythology to fill. A complete rewrite of the past.

Most importantly, cancel culture can destroy our children. Pamela B. Rutledge, Ph.D., wrote: "Being canceled can disman-

---

2 See: "The Successor Ideology," a Zoom podcast with Manhattan Institute President Reihan Salam, City Journal contributing editor Coleman Hughes, New York Times opinion columnist Ross Douthat, and columnist for Tablet Magazine, Wesley Yang.

3 Tom Cotton, "Cotton Takes on Cancel Culture," speech delivered June 12, 2020.

4 President Donald Trump speaking at Mount Rushmore, July 4, 2020.

5 President Barack Obama, in an interview about youth activism at an Obama Foundation Summit, October 2020.

tle a teen's entire social network. It isn't just missing Friday night's party. It is becoming an object of scorn. Teens will tell you, once you're canceled, it can be hard to come back. No one questions what actions got you canceled, but everyone worries about being connected to you in case they become canceled, too."[6]

In short, cancel culture leads to isolation which results in loneliness and there is a clear association between loneliness and mental illness, suicidal ideation and suicide itself.[7]

Let me be clear: Cancel culture is contributing to the rise of mental illness, suicidal ideation and suicide in our children.

Cancel culture has no use for the individual. Instead of uniting behind the social contract, the general will and the COMMON good, cancel culture is intent upon dividing us into competing tribes: divide and conquer. It feels as if cancel culture hit us head-on without mercy and has met little resistance.

Cancel culture is removing Black History!

Cancel culture is also in the business of "linguistic engineering." Which words are correct and which others must be eviscerated. I wrote about the attack on the N-word many years ago. It is a derogatory word. Like Mick and Jap and Wop and Kike. But it is one word, six letters, with a 400-year history. A history of slavery, civil war, Jim Crow and civil rights. Books that tell the story of slavery are attacked and removed from libraries because of that one word. Yet, it is a word that is thrown about in rap music constantly. We walk on dangerous ground when we attack language.

The souls of black people have been under attack in many different ways, but one of the most hurtful has been with language. And there is one word that is particularly painful. It be-

---

6 Pamela B. Rutledge, "Cancel Culture: Accountability or Bullying?," *Psychology Today*, March 3, 2021.

7 Beutel ME, Klein EM, Brähler E, et al. "Loneliness in the general population: prevalence, determinants and relations to mental health," *BMC Psychiatry*, March 20, 2017.

gins with "N." We can't say it or write it anymore. It is being removed from books that are considered classics, books that speak to us through time about a particular epoch when freedom was a gift of the "privileged" that came with being born white.

I fear removing this word will distort history. There are words that carry within them years of haunting memory. Nazi comes to mind. No need to say more. We know the history embedded in those four letters. If we removed the word from the lexicon to protect the feelings of those who experienced Nazism, we would do a disservice to their descendants—victims and victimizers.

This six-letter word is an icon that is slowly being removed from the culture. It speaks to us from an earlier age—the age of slavery—when the treatment of black people was inhuman. That icon immediately brings to mind a myriad of emotions, a plethora of pictures reminding us of the dehumanization, denigration and humiliation of a group of people, not for anything said or done, but merely for being black.

The "N" word, like Nazi, carries within it a history of man's inhumanity to man. It screams to us about the arrogance of white people who considered themselves to be entitled to an intrinsic value not to be accorded to those not white. It has been, pardon the expression, whitewashed. Not to protect the sensibilities of the black population, I fear, but to assuage the shame of the white people. By stripping it down to a letter, it loses its power as a symbol of an age of horror, almost presaging the twentieth-century Aryan moral depravity.

Watching *Django Unchained* and *Twelve Years a Slave* led me to believe that removing the word from classics that spoke of and documented that time was in the best interests of the white world, not those of colour, and certainly not those whose families were abused by slavery.

The word with six letters—a word I cannot write—is the word that represented a time that gave Lincoln the moral courage to push through the Thirteenth Amendment. This is the word that propelled Dr. Martin Luther King Jr. to speak of his dreams.

I think we need to keep that word to remind us of the importance of education, teaching morals and values that hold high the sanctity of all life—no matter the race, colour, creed or religion. It is learning about "the other" in order to make "the other" an "us." History proves this isn't easy. But I think that removing the symbols of that hate too soon can be counter-productive.

Turning the six-letter word I cannot write into the "N" word is an attempt to remove the guilt and shame that should still be felt by white culture. We need powerful symbols to remind us that we are all God's children, equal in His eyes and deserving of respect.

I worry that either removing removing the six-letter word from books or changing it to the acceptable "N" word could lead to wiping out the history of the moral and ethical failure it carries.

Imagine a little girl four generations from now reading *The Adventures of Tom Sawyer* and *Adventures of Huckleberry Finn*. She looks to her mother and says, "Mommy, what does the 'N' word mean?"

"The 'N' word? O, yes, I think I remember. I don't remember the word itself, but I do remember it means something terrible."

We must protect language to protect history.

We are colluding in the spread of cancel culture with silence, often out of fear. And that fear could lead to the downfall of our hard-fought for way of life. While Western Culture is firmly rooted in the Judeo-Christian ethic, cancel culture is firmly rooted in Critical Race Theory.

The late great journalist, George Jonas, wrote "Don't let Western civilization — the best and most humane form of civilization developed by mankind — perish by default."[8]

---

8 George Jonas, "The 10 Commandments of sending your troops to war," *National Post*, April 12, 2011.

8

Critical Race Theory

At its essence, Christianity is a belief in salvation, love, redemption, and forgiveness. At its essence, CRT is about classification, vilification, repudiation, and being unforgiving.[1]
—Jack Fowler, Vice President of *National Review*

C RITICAL RACE THEORY is defined by the *Encyclopedia Britannica* as the concept in which race is a socially constructed category ingrained in American law intended to maintain social, economic, and political inequalities between whites and non-whites. It holds that the U.S. society is inherently or systemically racist and that "the law and legal institutions in the United States are inherently racist insofar as they function to create and maintain social, economic, and political inequalities between whites and non-whites, especially African Americans."[2] CRT scholars allege many societal problems are rooted in the country's white majority using laws and other power to suppress the non-white population, whether consciously or subconsciously.

Critical Race Theory seems to have jumped on center stage from out of nowhere, but it had been incubating:

---

1 Jack Fowler, "Another Prestigious School Pummeled by Critical Race Theory," *National Review*, April 28, 2021.

2 https://www.britannica.com/topic/critical-race-theory/Basic-tenets-of-critical-race-theory.

CRT gradually proliferated in recent decades through academia, government structures, school systems, and the corporate world. It redefines human history as a struggle between the "oppressors" (white people) and the "oppressed" (everybody else), similarly to Marxism's reduction of history to a struggle between the "bourgeois" and the "proletariat." It labels institutions that emerged in majority-white societies as racist and "white supremacist."[3]

Marxism has been with us for more than 100 years, always trying to find a home. A home where it can destroy the culture. In 1918, there were two very prominent Marxists thinkers: Antonio Gramsci and Georg Lukács. Lukács realized that if the family unit and sexual morals were eroded, society could be broken down.[4] I think the question we fail to ask is: Why? Why would anyone agree to destroy the family unit, the smallest and most basic unit of authority in a society? He sought to promote radical sexual licence in the name of "freedom." He implemented a policy he titled "cultural terrorism," targeting children's minds through lectures that encouraged them to deride and reject traditional Judeo-Christian ethics.

In these lectures, graphic sexual matter was presented to children, and they were taught about loose sexual conduct. These teachings go back to pre-Judaism, before the revolutionary ethic demanded restraint on one's sexual desires and that children were not to be sexually used.

But that was not enough. His theory was that everyone in society was psychologically oppressed by the institutions of Western culture. Let's think about that for a moment. Of all the cultures that existed in the 1930s, Lukács looked around and decided that Western Culture was evil. Not the honor/shame cultures in Muslim countries or the caste system in India. Well, Freud did point out the need for repressing some of one's behaviours in order to fit in society. Western culture requires re-

---

3 Petr Svab, "Republican States Push Back Against Critical Race Theory," *The Epoch Times*, March 31, 2021.

4 See: David Galland, "The Birth of Cultural Marxism: How the 'Frankfurt School' Changed America," *Sagacious News*, August 16, 2016.

pressing one's sexual desires, the desire for revenge, the entitlement to steal, the love of gossip. I suppose one could say that Lukács wanted to free us from that "repression."

To teach this theory, Lukács helped implement the Frankfurt School which originated in Germany, but, irony of ironies, had to move to America when the Nazis overran Germany in 1934. The school was reborn at Columbia University, where its members began to exert their ideas on American culture.

The school published a plethora of material. The first of these was Critical Theory.

Critical Theory is a play on semantics—the meaning of words. "The theory was simple: criticize every pillar of Western culture—family, democracy, common law, freedom of speech, and others. The hope was that these pillars would crumble under the pressure."[5] Critical theory wants us to believe that objective truth does not exist, but our beliefs are simply "social constructions" resulting in morally equivalent narratives.

The Frankfurt School deconstructed the meaning of everything we believed. The meaning of race, sex and gender; and all people were divided into two new groups: the oppressors and the victims. Who wants to be a victim? It seems many want that designation as it takes away personal responsibility. It takes us back to the Garden of Eden where God provided everything, where Adam and Eve could be perennial children. When they were expelled, all of mankind had to take on personal responsibility.

Today, Critical Theory has morphed into Critical Race Theory.

For Critical Race Theory to take hold, one has to believe that "truth" does not exist, that everything we believe is a "social construct" resulting in a "narrative" and that "alternate narratives" are of equal value. At least at first, until alternate narratives are erased. Removing facts makes it easier to manipulate emotions.

Legal scholar Angela Harris explains Critical Race Theory in her foreword to *Critical Race Theory: An Introduction*:

---

5 Ibid.

Unlike traditional civil rights discourse, which stresses incrementalism and step-by-step progress, critical race theory questions the very foundations of the liberal order, including equality theory, legal reasoning, Enlightenment rationalism, and neutral principles of constitutional law.[6]

The World Economic Forum (WEF) has now weighed in on Critical Race Theory. The WEF defines CRT as a legal theory, arguing that "laws, rules, and regulations that govern society today have been shaped by the historical subordination of people of color, and that this is a driving force behind racial inequality today."[7]

It is also "a way of thinking about America's history through the lens of racism. It examines how the legacy of slavery and segregation in the US is embedded in modern-day legal systems and policies. And is the idea that racism is not a matter of individual bigotry but is systemic in America."[8]

According to the WEF, "Critical race theory tells a story about institutionalized racial disadvantage and systemic racial inequality. It examines how the legacy of slavery and segregation in the US is embedded in modern-day legal systems and policies." And insists "there is a profound sense of urgency for companies to actively work to tackle inequality and the inequity that follows as a result."[9]

The WEF says this systemic racism began when Africa was colonized by Europeans.

Religion and education were tools to achieve systemic social control and to build communities of local labourers to advance economic development in the colonies. The legacy of that subjugation is still witnessed today in post-co-

6 Angela Harris, Foreword to *Critical Race Theory: An Introduction*, Richard Delgado and Jean Stefancic eds., NYU Press, 2017.

7 See the World Economic Forum video here: https://twitter.com/wef/status/1491094355444219906.

8 Juliet Masiga, WEF Digital Editor, "What is critical race theory?" *World Economic Forum*, February 10, 2022.

9 Ibid.

lonial systems which perpetuate the exploitative practices and institutions that underpinned a distorted social contract. A contract that was -- and continues to be -- steeped in inequality.

A similar pattern played out in the African diaspora, notably within North America's Black communities, where critical race theory 'tells a story about institutionalized racial disadvantage and systemic racial inequality' within a societal construct that has historically characterized Blacks as less deserving of the full privileges of 'civilization'.[10]

The WEF points to the high incarceration rate among black Americans to make its point about systemic racism.

Take the US criminal justice system, for example. While everyone is seen as equal under the law, Black Americans are imprisoned at 5 times the rate of white people. CRT says this disparity is a legacy of America's racist past.[11]

Why should anyone care about the opinions of the WEF and its chairman, Klaus Schwab? They provided the world with the Great Reset plan in June 2020. Ivan Wecke explains:

The idea is that global capitalism should be transformed so that corporations no longer focus solely on serving shareholders but become custodians of society by creating value for customers, suppliers, employees, communities and other 'stakeholders'. The way the WEF sees stakeholder capitalism being carried out is through a range of 'multi-stakeholder partnerships' bringing together the private sector, governments and civil society across all areas of global governance.[12]

---

10 See the World Economic Forum video here: https://twitter.com/wef/status/1491094355444219906.

11 Ibid.

12 Ivan Wecke, "Conspiracy theories aside, there is something fishy about the Great Reset," *Open Society*, August 16, 2021.

In reality, this means giving corporations more power over society, and democratic institutions less. In the WEF's vision, "the government voice would be one among many, without always being the final arbiter."[13] Governments would be just one stakeholder in a multi-stakeholder model of global governance. Harris Gleckman, senior fellow at the University of Massachusetts, describes the WEF report as:

> [T]he most comprehensive proposal for re-designing global governance since the formulation of the United Nations during World War II.
> (...)
> WEF partners include some of the biggest companies in oil (Saudi Aramco, Shell, Chevron, BP), food (Unilever, The Coca-Cola Company, Nestlé), technology (Facebook, Google, Amazon, Microsoft, Apple) and pharmaceuticals (AstraZeneca, Pfizer, Moderna).
>
> Instead of corporations serving many stakeholders, in the multi-stakeholder model of global governance, corporations are promoted to being official stakeholders in global decision-making, while governments are relegated to being one of many stakeholders. In practice, corporations become the main stakeholders, while governments take a backseat role, and civil society is mainly window dressing.[14]

I suggest that if the WEF gets its way, US education will be decided by them and not the American people. Bari Weiss, former writer at the *New York Times* stated the following:

> Critical race theory says there is no such thing as neutrality, not even in the law, which is why the very notion of colorblindness—the Kingian dream of judging people not

---

13 WEF Report: *Everybody's Business: Strengthening International Cooperation in a More Interdependent World.* https://www3.weforum.org/docs/WEF_GRI_EverybodysBusiness_Report_2010.pdf.

14 Ivan Wecke, "Conspiracy theories aside, there is something fishy about the Great Reset," *Open Society*, August 16, 2021.

based on the color of their skin but by the content of their character—must itself be deemed racist. Racism is no longer about individual discrimination. It is about systems that allow for disparate outcomes among racial groups. If everyone doesn't finish the race at the same time, then the course must have been flawed and should be dismantled. (...)

In fact, any feature of human existence that creates disparity of outcomes must be eradicated: The nuclear family, politeness, even rationality itself can be defined as inherently racist or evidence of white supremacy, as a Smithsonian institution suggested this summer. The KIPP charter schools[15] recently eliminated the phrase "work hard" from its famous motto "Work Hard. Be Nice." because the idea of working hard "supports the illusion of meritocracy."[16]

In her letter of resignation from the *New York Times,* Ms. Weiss wrote:

> But the lessons that ought to have followed the election (2020)—lessons about the importance of understanding other Americans, the necessity of resisting tribalism, and the centrality of the free exchange of ideas to a democratic society—have not been learned. Instead, a new consensus has emerged in the press, but perhaps especially at this paper: that truth isn't a process of collective discovery, but an orthodoxy already known to an enlightened few whose job is to inform everyone else.

> Twitter is not on the masthead of The New York Times. But Twitter has become its ultimate editor. As the ethics and mores of that platform have become those of the paper, the paper itself has increasingly become a kind of performance space. Stories are chosen and told in a way to satisfy the narrowest of audiences, rather than to allow a curious public to read about the world and then draw their own conclusions. I was always taught that journalists were charged with writing the first rough draft of history.

---

15 See: https://www.kipp.org/schools/.

16 Bari Weiss, "Stop Being Shocked," *Tablet,* October 14, 2020.

Now, history itself is one more ephemeral thing molded to fit the needs of a predetermined narrative.[17]

The failure of mainstream media to be unbiased reporters of the facts has contributed to the growing "woke" culture, to the rise in Critical Race Theory and groupthink—the undermining of the individual.

We know for certain that Critical Race Theory has taken hold, because the venerated American Medical Association also promotes aspects of CRT.

The American Medical Association has produced a 54-page document called *Advancing Health Equity: A Guide to Language, Narrative, and Concepts*.[18] Sally Sartel dissects it:

> The guide condemns several "dominant narratives" in medicine. One is the "narrative of individualism," and its misbegotten corollary, the notion that health is a personal responsibility. A more "equitable narrative," the guide instructs, would "expose the political roots underlying apparently 'natural' economic arrangements, such as property rights, market conditions, gentrification, oligopolies and low wage rates." The dominant narratives, says the AMA, "create harm, undermining public health and the advancement of health equity; they must be named, disrupted, and corrected.

> One form of correction that the AMA recommends is "equity explicit" language. Instead of "individuals," doctors should say "survivors"; instead of "marginalized communities," they should say, "groups that are struggling against economic marginalization." We must also be clear that "people are not vulnerable, they are made vulnerable." Accordingly, we should replace the statement, "Low-income people have the highest level of coronary artery disease," with "People underpaid and forced into poverty as a result of banking policies, real estate developers gentrifying neighborhoods, and corporations weakening the power

---

17 Bari Weiss, "Resignation Letter," *Bariweiss.com*, July 14, 2020.

18 https://www.ama-assn.org/system/files/ama-aamc-equity-guide.pdf.

of labor movements, among others, have the highest level of coronary artery disease.[19]

John Murawski, a reporter whose work has been published in the *Wall Street Journal, Washington Times* and the *Toronto Star,* noted how medical schools are lecturing future doctors about intersectionality, implicit bias, identity, oppression, power and privilege:

> In the wake of the COVID-19 pandemic and the George Floyd killing by a Minneapolis cop, medical researchers have seized on systemic racism as a unifying theory that explains the shorter life expectancies and more prevalent chronic conditions among black Americans. The mass conversion to systemic racism as the canonical explanation for health disparities has swept through the medical profession with stunning velocity, emboldening scholarship with the certitude of a single explanatory narrative.[20]

John D. Sailer writes:

> The University of California–Davis School of Medicine has developed a mandatory anti-racism course and introduced a webinar series with talks on "Addressing Structural Racism" and "Moving from Ally to Advocate." At Louisiana State University Health Shreveport School of Medicine, faculty must undergo annual training on cultural sensitivity, diversity, and bias. The University of Minnesota School of Medicine collaborates on its curriculum with the Medical Education Reform Student Coalition (MERSC), an offshoot of the activist organization White Coats 4 Black Lives.
> (...)
> The Liaison Committee on Medical Education (LCME) accredits medical schools in the United States, and has

19 Sally Sartel, "What is Happening to My Profession?," *Quillette*, November 30, 2021.

20 John Murawski, "Medical Journals Pour Forth Hundreds of Articles on Race and Racism," *Real Clear Investigations*, November 11, 2021.

long required schools to bolster student and faculty diversity and teach cultural competence.

(...)

The Oregon Health and Science University, ranked first in the nation for family medicine, was reaccredited in the summer of 2020, but the LCME found it "unsatisfactory" in the area of "faculty diversity." In response, the school's senior associate dean for education promised a "concerted effort and sustained commitment at the highest levels of the institution."

> In November, OHSU adopted a 24-page Diversity, Equity, Inclusion and Anti-Racism Strategic Action Plan, created "in alignment with accreditation requirements." The new plan makes it virtually impossible for faculty to object to DEI measures without jeopardizing their careers. It institutes ongoing training on "DEI and anti-racism" with "consequences for individuals who are not compliant with the required training." It also mandates new performance reviews that evaluate "how the employee is contributing to improving DEI, anti-racism and social justice," along with a social justice section in faculty promotion packages, again reinforced with unelaborated "consequences." The school even issued its own Inclusive Language Guide, with a long glossary including entries for "Karen," "Ken," "whiteness," "micro-invalidation," and "white fragility."[21]

These teachings go against the guidelines shared by many medical colleges which speak of patients as individuals, not part of a particular group. Here are some guidelines from The Ontario College of Physicians and Surgeons:

> The College does not view CPGs (guidelines) as rules 'cast in stone,' but rather as important resources, which will provide physicians with a range of appropriate options for patient care, based on available research data and professional consensus.
>
> (...)

---

21 John D. Sailer, "First, Brook No Dissent," *City Journal*, March 15, 2022.

Typically, CPGs are intended to provide physicians with a framework for diagnosing, assessing and treating clinical conditions commonly encountered in practice.

Because CPGs are developed to promote best practice for populations of patients, they will have variable applicability to individual patients. They do not define a standard of care, but may inform the standard of care.[22]

The Critical Race Theory (CRT) movement officially organized itself in 1989, at the first annual Workshop on Critical Race Theory, though its intellectual origins go back much further, to the 1960s and '70s. I suggest Critical Race Theory has been designed to turn non-Black people into victimizers while encouraging Black and Indigenous People of Color (BIPOC) to be the forever victims. It is dehumanizing, demeaning and worst of all, infantilizing an entire group of people based on skin color. This is culturally acquired psychosis at work.

There is another term for this type of victimhood: ressentiment defined as "the psychology of blame" that comes to us from Nietzsche (the man who declared that God is dead). Ressentiment is a sense of hostility directed toward an object that one identifies as the cause of one's frustration, that is, an assignment of blame for one's frustration. "It's not my fault." The sense of weakness in the face of the "cause" generates a rejecting/justifying value system—a malignant morality "which attacks or denies the perceived source of one's frustration. This value system prevents the resentful individual from addressing and overcoming their insecurities and flaws."[23] Once again, "It's not my fault." Ressentiment is an influential force for the creation of identity, for one can be defined by what one opposes and fights against.

Today's progressives are actively promoting this negative philosophy which is adding to a new culturally acquired psy-

---

22   https://www.cpso.on.ca/Physicians/Policies-Guidance/Statements-Positions/Clinical-Practice-Guidelines.

23   See: https://en.wikipedia.org/wiki/Ressentiment.

chosis in our communities. Los Angeles lawyer David Pivtorak is quoted as saying:

> Critical race theory is a Trojan horse of sorts. It disguises itself as the gold standard of fairness and justice but, in fact, relies on vilification and the idea of permanent oppressor and oppressed races. Its goal is not ensuring that all people play by the same rules, regardless of race, but equity, which is a euphemism for race-based outcomes.[24]

Crystal Raypole, a freelance writer for *Healthline Media,* noted:

> The idea of the victim mentality is spread a great deal in pop culture and casual conversation to refer to people who seem to wallow in negativity and force it upon others. The victim mentality rests on three key beliefs: Bad things happen and will keep happening; other people or circumstances are to blame; any efforts to create change will fail, so there's no point in trying.[25]

That reeks of helplessness and hopelessness which are the precursors of mental illness. Raypole continues:

> People who feel trapped in a state of victimization often *do* express a lot of negativity, but it's important to realize significant pain and distress often fuel this mindset.

They place blame elsewhere. They make excuses. They do not take responsibility. They react to most life hurdles with, "It's not my fault."

> People who come from a place of victimization may show little interest in trying to make changes. They may reject offers of help, and it may seem like they're only interested in feeling sorry for themselves.

---

24 In "Critical Race Theory Is About to Face Its Day(s) in Court" by John Murawski, *The Epoch Times,* April 27, 2021.

25 Crystal Raypole, "How to Identify and Deal with a Victim Mentality," *Healthline,* December 11, 2019.

Over time, negative self-talk can damage resilience, making it harder to bounce back from challenges and heal.

A victim mentality can take a toll on emotional well-being. People with this mindset might feel frustrated and angry with a world that seems against them; hopeless about their circumstances never changing; hurt when they believe loved ones don't care, and resentful of people who seem happy and successful.

These emotions can weigh heavily on people who believe they'll always be victims, building and festering when they aren't addressed. Over time, these feelings might contribute to angry outbursts, depression, isolation and loneliness.[26]

I suggest that the Black, Indigenous, and People of Color (BIPOC) are as much victims of bullying as those whom their "leaders" are bullying into silence with calls of racism as they demand the implementation of CRT-justified discrimination. They are told incessantly that their failures are not their own—that it is systemic racism that is holding them back. They are eternal victims and can be no other.

Let's talk about systemic racism and racial equity

Let's talk about systemic racism.

What is it, exactly? I looked at many sources. First, it seems, we must learn the meaning of structural racism. Here is the explanation from the *Aspen Institute*:

> Structural Racism: A system in which public policies, institutional practices, cultural representations, and other norms work in various, often reinforcing ways to perpetuate racial group inequity. It identifies dimensions of our history and culture that have allowed privileges associated with "whiteness" and disadvantages associated with "col-

---

26 Ibid.

or" to endure and adapt over time. Structural racism is not something that a few people or institutions choose to practice. Instead it has been a feature of the social, economic and political systems in which we all exist.[27]

Systemic racism, as defined by the *Cambridge Dictionary,* is the result of "policies and practices that exist throughout a whole society or organization, and that result in and support a continued unfair advantage to some people and unfair or harmful treatment of others based on race."[28]

The Office of the United Nations High Commissioner for Human Rights states:

'Systemic racism' can be defined as an infrastructure of rulings, ordinances or statutes promulgated by a sovereign government or authoritative entity, whereas such ordinances and statutes entitles one ethnic group in a society certain rights and privileges, while denying other groups in that society these same rights and privileges because of long-established cultural prejudices, religious prejudices, fears, myths, and Xenophobia's (sic) held by the entitled group.

In the year 2020, there exists no U.S. federal government or state government statutes or ordinances that will accommodate systemic racism. However, this by no means is to suggest that racism is not prevalent in America today.[29]

But NAACP President Derrick Johnson defined systemic racism as "systems and structures that have procedures or processes that disadvantages African Americans."[30]

Glenn Harris, president of Race Forward and publisher of

27 https://www.aspeninstitute.org/blog-posts/structural-racism-definition/.

28 https://dictionary.cambridge.org/dictionary/english/systemic-racism.

29 https://www.ohchr.org/Documents/Issues/Racism/WGEAPD/Session27/submissions-statements/mdshahid-systemicracism.pdf.

30 N'dea Yancey-Bragg, "What is systemic racism? Here's what it means and how you can help dismantle it," *USA Today,* June 15, 2020.

Colorlines, defined it as "the complex interaction of culture, policy and institutions that holds in place the outcomes we see in our lives," and "Systemic racism is naming the process of white supremacy."[31]

In many ways, "systemic racism" and "structural racism" are synonymous. If there is a difference between the terms, it can be said to exist in the fact that a structural racism analysis pays more attention to the historical, cultural and social psychological aspects of our currently racialized society. Then there is racial equity. Again from the Aspen Institute:

> Racial equity refers to what a genuinely non-racist society would look like. In a racially equitable society, the distribution of society's benefits and burdens would not be skewed by race. In other words, racial equity would be a reality in which a person is no more or less likely to experience society's benefits or burdens just because of the color of their skin. This is in contrast to the current state of affairs in which a person of color is more likely to live in poverty, be imprisoned, drop out of high school, be unemployed and experience poor health outcomes like diabetes, heart disease, depression and other potentially fatal diseases. Racial equity holds society to a higher standard. It demands that we pay attention not just to individual-level discrimination, but to overall social outcomes.[32]

That is a lot to overcome.

How many BIPOC would never have thought of themselves as victims of oppression without the leadership that reminds them of their victimhood every day? Leadership, moreover, that does not appear to believe a word they say?

If skin color is the defining characteristic for success or failure, and BIPOC are at the mercy of their skin color, how is it that Patrisse Cullors, a self-proclaimed "trained Marxist"[33]

---

31 Ibid.

32 https://www.aspeninstitute.org/wp-content/uploads/files/content/docs/rcc/RCC-Structural-Racism-Glossary.pdf.

33 Yaron Steinbuch, "Black Lives Matter co-founder describes herself as

and one of three activists who cofounded Black Lives Matter in 2013, owns several properties with her spouse, BLM Canada cofounder Janaya Khan? They own four homes purchased over the course of five years: a three-bed, one-and-a-half-bath Inglewood home for $510,000 in 2016; a four-bedroom residence in South L.A. for $590,000 in 2018; a three-bedroom home on several acres in the Atlanta suburb of Conyers for $415,000 in 2020; and, most recently, the Topanga "compound."[34]

Journalist Jasmyne A. Cannick defended Cullors: "Nowhere is it written that if you care about and fight for Black lives that you have to live in squalor and poverty. That you are not allowed to get educated and move up in the world." Cannick also stated, "What's not being talked about is the fact that she actually works. That she has jobs. Jobs that pay her and just like you or me would do, she's investing her money and taking care of her family."[35]

But she said that black and brown people are at the mercy of their skin color. For someone who promotes systemic racism and the unfairness of being black, she has done well. How did she overcome being black? How does she square that circle? If she can succeed, why can't other black people succeed?

Sadly, this focus on race is harming the most vulnerable: our children. Here are some terms used by parents:

> Racially divisive curriculum, blatant activism in the classroom, infantilization of students and staff of color, sanctioned discrimination, radical gender ideology and racist poison.[36]

Daniel Greenfield, Shillman Fellow at the David Horowitz Freedom Center, warned that systemic racism has become a cult.

'trained Marxist,'" *New York Post*, June 25, 2020.

34 Ian Spiegelman, "Inside the Uproar Over Patrisse Cullors's Real Estate Holdings," *Los Angeles Magazine*, April 16, 2021.

35 Jasmyne A. Cannick, "Stop Helping White Supremacists Attack Black Women," on her personal blog, April 13, 2021.

36 Erika Sanzi, "The Coming Bipartisan Backlash to Public School Wokeness," *Newsweek*, April 20, 2021.

Like any state cult, it's taught in schools, mandated in government offices, and the faithful spread it through every organization. Faith in critical race theory is becoming a prerequisite for public service and public life. A failure to pay tribute to its tenets, to acknowledge your racism, to 'lean in', and promise to 'do better' is heresy.[37]

Not all people of color are leaning in. A parent, Ndona Muboyayi, recently told Conor Friedersdorf of *The Atlantic* the following story about her son:

My children have always been so proud of who they are. Then all of a sudden they started to question themselves because of what they were taught...My son has wanted to be a lawyer since he was 11. Then one day he came home and told me, 'But Mommy, there are these systems put in place that prevent Black people from accomplishing anything.' That's what they're teaching Black kids: that all of this time for the past 400 years, this is what [white people have] done to you and your people. The narrative is, "You can't get ahead."
(...)
One day my daughter told me she was taught that all white people are privileged and part of a system of white supremacy. My son said the same thing.
(...)
I am aware that there are parents who are very negative and teach negative things to their children. And if a child does have a thought that is negative, you correct them, but in a positive manner. You don't have to correct them by browbeating everyone and making them ashamed of who they are and telling them that because of how they look, they're innately bad.[38]

Ndona Muboyayi is not the only black parent to be concerned about the education system in her neighbourhood.

---

37 Daniel Greenfield, "Systemic Racism is a Conspiracy Theory Cult," *FrontPage Magazine*, April 15, 2021.
38 Conor Friedersdorf, "The Narrative Is, 'You Can't Get Ahead'," *The Atlantic*, April 3, 2021.

Like white families, black parents also feel fear speaking up. Muboyayi continues:

> You know, certain elements of our community are threatening to get people fired. Even if someone just poses a question, or expresses a conflicting view, you're immediately labeled a part of the problem, a white supremacist, and people will say, "Find out where they work."
>
> If you're a Black person who says what I say, you get attacked too. Now, I'm independent. I work for myself. So who is going to fire me? But what are we telling our children, who will one day lead our society, when we show them that if you pose a question, and if someone doesn't agree with you, maybe they're going to go after your job?[39]

BIPOC have been told over and over they are victims of racism. They have been bullied into this belief the same way that leaders of BLM and CRT have bullied non-coloured people to believe they are the cause of everything evil in America. Over time, these beliefs can become part of the collective unconscious, in Jungian terms, and what Oxford University biologist Richard Dawkins described as "cultural memes." He wrote there are two types of information that are intertwined and passed through the generations. There are the genes that pass on our DNA and there are "memes," which he refers to as "units of deep cultural information." These cultural memes become as much a part of us as our DNA which dictates the color of our eyes. In other words, in time, white people will innately know they are oppressors and BIPOC will know they are victims of oppression.

And then there are "grandiose infantile delusions of entitlement." What a spectacular expression! I first learned it in the 1990s when I took my 2000-hour residency in clinical pastoral education to be a hospital chaplain. And here we are in the 2020s, and the entitlement has expanded. Now calls for equity include calls for the right to free stuff: education, healthcare,

---

39 Ibid.

housing, food and a get out of jail free card. My, my, aren't we so entitled!

And back to Critical Race Theory

This entitlement has taken on a more sinister meaning because of Critical Race Theory and diversity politics. Only some people are entitled. Critical Race Theory (CRT) holds the view that the law and legal institutions are inherently racist and that race itself, instead of being biologically grounded and natural, is a socially constructed concept that is used by white people to further their economic and political interests at the expense of people of colour. According to CRT, racial inequality emerges from the social, economic, and legal differences that white people create between "races" to maintain elite white interests in labour markets and politics, giving rise to poverty and criminality in many minority communities. If one teaches that race is a social construct, the problems are not moral and thus the fault of the individual; rather, they are systemic and the fault of the entire culture which must therefore be destroyed.

Promoting this ideology requires canceling the past, as Joseph Pearce, author and senior contributor at *The Imaginative Conservative*, explained:

> [C]ritical race theory is as obsessed with race as were the Nazis. According to the new generation of Marxists, the political struggle is not about class war but race war; it's not about a struggle between the classes but a struggle between the races. Like the Nazis, the critical race theorists don't believe that racism is a prejudice in individuals but is something determined by history. It is not something evil in the heart of men but something systemic in history itself. Since this is so, the solution is not teaching and preaching the love of neighbour but the destruction of the "system." And since the "system" is history itself, the final solution is the cancelling of the past, the utter erasing of the collective cultural memory of the people.[40]

---

40 Joseph Pearce, "When Hitler Seduces Marx," *The Imaginative Conserva-*

But what happens when we erase the collective cultural memory of the people? What happens when we know longer know the great names of the past?

Shall we remove the names of the Founding Fathers of their countries? In the United States of America, the Founding Fathers—George Washington, Benjamin Franklin, Thomas Jefferson—loom large in the psyche of the people. They are wrapped in legend and mythologized. They are entwined with the Declaration of Independence and the Constitution, the documents that comprise the creation story of America.

Attacks are being made against statues of these people.

What would happen if the names on these documents were removed? When the Supreme Court makes rulings, it refers to the Constitution and to the Founders in order to provide an historical perspective that adds legitimacy to their decision-making. If the Founders are removed, there is a good possibility that over time the laws will lose their legitimacy, because when a ruling is given, one could simply respond, "Who says?"

Moses Mendelssohn (1729–1786), a noted German philosopher and the grandfather of composer Felix Mendelssohn, wrote that historical truths and events are only witnessed once. We learn of them through those who pass down the information. "Hence the respectability and the trustworthiness of the narrator constitute the sole evidence of historical matters. Without testimony, we cannot be convinced of any historical truth. Without authority, the truth of history vanishes with the occurrence itself."[41]

Without a past, there is no future greatness.

Morality forces us to make decisions based on the eternal values—goodness, truth and beauty. Morality is the belief that some behaviour is right and acceptable (in accordance with God's will and in harmony with the eternal values) and that other behaviour is wrong (a rejection of the divine will). We then make choices regarding our behaviour based on the

---

tive, April 30, 2021.

41 Moses Mendelssohn quoted in *The Jews: A Treasury of Art and Literature*, Sharon Keller, editor, Beaux Arts Editions, 1992, p. 161.

morals taught in the ethic. The moral value of the Judeo-Christian ethic which underpins the West tells us that all people are born with equal intrinsic value. When that ethic is erased, our decisions will have to be made based on another morality. And, the morals and values imbued in CRT tell us that our lives are predicted on skin color. In other words, the moral choices you make will have no effect on your life.

Critical Race Theory is also changing math.

Math, once a language of absolutes, has been refitted for non-white people. In Oregon, educators know that there isn't "only one right way" to learn math, and it should not center on "Western, Eurocentric ways of processing and knowing information. When students are required to learn in this way, they either have to unlearn their learned native traditions to meet teacher expectations, or they are deprived of learning math in their ancestral history."[42] Educators learn that math should not be taught in a linear fashion but as a "web," and that objectivity should not be reinforced. Educators should employ "learning webs that connect content."

The state of Virginia was seeking to eliminate special courses in advanced mathematics for high school students before the 11th grade.[43] I wonder how bridges, buildings and airplanes will turn out in the future.

Educators are told not to grade, saying that it's racist, because grading practices are "focused on lack of knowledge," saying that this reinforces "perfectionism." Students should not be graded, the workbook states, on "procedural or skills-based knowledge" but on "conceptual knowledge." Also, asking students to "show their work" is racist; white supremacy, because maybe they solved the problem some other more intuitive way.[44]

---

42 Jake Dima, "Oregon promoting teacher course on 'dismantling racism in mathematics'," *Washington Examiner*, February 12, 2021.

43 Sam Dorman, "Virginia moving to eliminate all accelerated math courses before 11th grade as part of equity-focused plan," *Fox News*, April 22, 2021.

44 Libby Emmons, "Oregon promotes divisive critical race theory in math curriculum," *The Post-Millennial*, February 15, 2021.

In New York, a college prep school sent white parents of children, from grade 6 to grade 12, literary materials asking them to identify their "level" of whiteness, ranging from "white supremacist" to "white abolitionist."

> The white parents were asked to work toward becoming white traitors and abolitionists by "subverting white authority" as well as "changing institutions, dismantling whiteness, and not allowing whiteness to reassert itself."

> The curriculum, authored by Barnor Hesse, an associate professor of African American studies, political science, and sociology at Northwestern University, weaponizes language such as "superiority" and "white regime" to challenge people who operate without fully acknowledging the "burden of Blackness."

> [He writes,] "There is a regime of whiteness, and there are action-oriented white identities. People who identify with whiteness are one of these. It's about time we build an ethnography of whiteness, since white people have been the ones writing about and governing Others."[45]

These "values" are victimizing and demeaning non-white people. One could make a case that they are being bullied. Black people just can't keep up with other people who are not black. How shameful and demeaning; one's color is the obstacle to success. How sad.

The most powerful exponent of this worldview is Ibram X. Kendi—who, it should be noted, now holds Elie Wiesel's old chair at Boston University. Elie Wiesel was liberated from Buchenwald in 1945 by advancing Allied troops and taken to Paris, where he studied at the Sorbonne and worked as a journalist. In 1958, he published his first book, *La Nuit* (*The Night*), a memoir of his experiences in a concentration camp. He has written nearly thirty books, some of which are based on those expe-

---

45 Jordan Boyd, "New York School Principal Urges Parents To Become 'White Abolitionists' With Propaganda Graphic," *The Federalist*, February 16, 2021.

rienced in the camp. In his many lectures, Wiesel concerned himself with the situation of the Jews and other groups who have suffered persecution and death because of their religion, race or national origin.

Kendi, however, believes "to be antiracist is to see all cultures in their differences as on the same level, as equals." He writes: "When we see cultural difference we are seeing cultural difference—nothing more, nothing less."[46] Notice that according to Kendi, it is *cultures* which are equal rather than individuals.

Bari Weiss responds: "It's hard to imagine that anyone could believe that cultures that condone honor killings of unchaste young women are 'nothing more, nothing less' than culturally different from our own."[47]

Or that a caste system that decides before you are born that you will always be searching for food in the garbage. Or cultures that value men more than women and condone the abortion of female fetuses.

Weiss continues, "But whether he believes it or not, it's obvious that embracing such relativism is a highly effective tool for ascension and seizing power."[48]

It was Franz Boas, in the early twentieth century, who brought us the term cultural relativism, suggesting that all cultures are equal. I wrote about this in my book, *Back to the Ethic Reclaiming Western Values*:

> We can look back to the early 20th century when Franz Boas brought forward his now well-known theory of cultural relativism which held that all cultures were essentially equal but simply had to be understood in their own terms. "Comparing two cultures was tantamount to comparing apples and oranges." This marked a decisive break with the evolutionary thinking of the period, which attempted to organize cultures and cultural artifacts by

---

46 See Goodreads quotes: https://www.goodreads.com/work/quotes/62549152-how-to-be-an-antiracist?page=3.

47 Bari Weiss, "Stop Being Shocked," *Tablet*, October 13, 2020.

48 Ibid.

an imagined level of progress. Boas was pushing back on the ethnocentrism; the practice of viewing and judging someone else's culture based on the values and beliefs of one's own.[49]

Boas promoted the idea that no culture is better than another or more evolved. He taught his views during his nearly four-decade career teaching anthropology at Columbia University (home to the Frankfurt School), where he built the first anthropology program in the country and trained the first generation of anthropologists in the U.S., who shared these views everywhere for decades.

If we follow his teachings, we must accept all values and all cultures into our Western societies, including those that attack our families and our institutions in the name of diversity, inclusivity, equity (DIE) or multiculturalism. That is taking place in America today.

But history has proven Boas completely wrong. After seeing the unspeakable savagery perpetrated by the Nazis, the Marxists, and the Islamist fundamentalists, no decent person is obligated to consider all cultures, all ideas, or all cultural practices as equals. We do not have to bow down before their idols, even when they are presented in the latest fashion of ideological clothing and by our own intellectuals.

Christopher Rufo, a senior fellow at the Manhattan Institute, writes:

> [Critical race theory] has increasingly become the default ideology in our public institutions over the past decade. It has been injected into government agencies, public school systems, teacher training programs, and corporate human-resources departments, in the form of diversity-training programs, human-resources modules, public-policy frameworks, and school curricula.
> (...)
> Indeed, critical race theorists explicitly reject equality—

---

49 Diane Bederman, *Back to the Ethic Reclaiming Western Values*, Mantua Books, 2015.

the principle proclaimed in the Declaration of Independence, defended in the Civil War, and codified into law with the Fourteenth and Fifteenth Amendments, the Civil Rights Act of 1964, and the Voting Rights Act of 1965. To them, equality represents 'mere nondiscrimination' and provides 'camouflage' for white supremacy, patriarchy, and oppression."[50]

Critical Race Theory is nothing more, nor less, than a divisive political ideology diametrically opposed to the concept of one nation, one people and the common good. It was Darwin who first suggested a mechanism for group selection by differentiating between tribes based on selfish individualism and tribes who believed in caring for others within the tribe. He wrote: "A tribe including many members who, from possessing in a high degree the spirit of patriotism, fidelity, obedience, courage, and sympathy, were always ready to give aid to each other and to sacrifice themselves for the common good, would be victorious over most other tribes and this would be natural selection."[51]

The Judeo-Christian ethic that underpins freedom in the West teaches us about caring for the other and to turn away from the "selfish gene" and the law of nature. To quote Rabbi Sacks, "In Homo sapiens a miracle of nature meets a miracle of culture: religion, which turns selfish genes into selfless people."[52]

Critical Race Theory and diversity politics are taking us back to a time of primitive tribalism, dividing us into two tribes based on racial identity: non-white, the permanently oppressed, and white, the eternal oppressor, promoting the "selfish gene" rather than the gene of compassion and cooperation.

---

50 Christopher Rufo, "The Courage of Our Convictions," *City Journal*, April 22, 2021.

51 Charles Darwin, *The Decent of Man*, Chapter 5, 1874. https://psychclassics.yorku.ca/Darwin/Descent/descent5.htm.

52 Rabbi Jonathan Sacks, "Darwin pointed the way to an unselfish evolution," *The Times*, March 27, 2009. https://www.rabbisacks.org/archive/darwin-pointed-way-unselfish-evolution/.

9

Revenge Racism

[A] man that studieth revenge, keeps his own wounds green,
which otherwise would heal, and do well.
—Francis Bacon, "On Revenge" (1625)

ODAY, WE ARE witnessing what I call Revenge Racism
promoted by leaders of Black Lives Matter, Critical Race
Theory and left-wing ideologues. As declared by Angela Harris
in her foreword to *Critical Race Theory: An Introduction*:

> Unlike traditional civil rights discourse, which stresses
> incrementalism and step-by-step progress, critical race
> theory questions the very foundations of the liberal order,
> including equality theory, legal reasoning, Enlightenment
> rationalism, and neutral principles of constitutional law.[1]

This is a full-frontal attack on western morals, values and
ethics that teach all people are born with equal intrinsic value—that we are defined by our character, not our superficial
characteristics.

Those who promote systemic racism are using old tactics
to promote the new. They "frame" a destructive policy as a vir-
tuous and humanitarian action with no hint of its very likely,

---

1 Angela Harris, Foreword to *Critical Race Theory: An Introduction*, Richard
Delgado and Jean Stefancic (Eds.), NYU Press, 2017.

if not intended, negative real world effects. These realities are not grasped by the public until the irreversible policy has been implemented and the horses are out of the barn. This is also referred to as "framing," used by the Tsarists and inherited and advanced as a "science" by Lenin, the NKVD and the KGB. Basically, they demonize an adversarial target, eliminate all negative information regarding their own favored position, and fabricate a library of positive information to sanitize, idealize and promote their ideas and values.

In America, as part of the nation's historic reckoning on racism, the American Psychological Association has apologized to communities of color for its role—and the role of the discipline of psychology—in contributing to "systemic racism."

> APA is profoundly sorry, accepts responsibility for, and owns the actions and inactions of APA itself, the discipline of psychology, and individual psychologists who stood as leaders for the organization and field.[2]

Psychoanalyst Dr. Donald Moss says people of no color, both children and adults, must now deal with the idea that simply being white is a mental condition that one acquires by being born Caucasian. This is racism on steroids. Dr. Moss, a private-practice psychoanalyst from New York, gives a presentation entitled "On Having Whiteness," which is targeted toward other psychoanalysts and social workers. In it, Moss argues that whiteness "is parasitic in that it is contagious, passed on by other infected people," and that "biologically 'white' people have a particular susceptibility to 'Whiteness.'"[3]

In 2020, "On Having Whiteness" was a plenary address for the South African Psychoanalytical Association. South Africa! A country that pulled itself away from apartheid, the Afrikaans name given by the white-ruled South African Nationalist Party

---

2 "APA apologizes for longstanding contributions to systemic racism," *American Psychological Association*, October 29, 2021.
3 James Murphy, "Psychoanalyst Explains That 'Whiteness' Is a 'Malignant and Parasitic-like Condition,'" *New American*, January 20, 2020.

in 1948 to the country's harsh, institutionalized system of racial segregation. It came to an end in the early 1990s in a series of steps that led to the formation of a democratic government in 1994. Those steps began with Nelson Mandela, a man who had been jailed for 27 years and was freed in 1990. He negotiated the end of apartheid in South Africa, bringing peace to a racially divided country and leading the fight for human rights around the world. He brought peace to a "racially divided" country. And what is "On Having Whiteness" doing? It is racially dividing a country once again, while spreading the hate elsewhere.

> According to the description for the presentation, "Parasitic Whiteness renders its hosts' appetites voracious, insatiable, and perverse; these deformed appetites particularly target non-white people; and once established, these appetites are nearly impossible to eliminate."

> (...) Moss does have a treatment for the scourge of Whiteness: "Effective treatment requires a combination of psychological and social-historical interventions, which can reasonably aim only to reshape whiteness' infiltrated appetites — to reduce their intensities, to redistribute their aims, and to occasionally turn those aims toward the work of reparation."

> So, if you suffer from "whiteness," you can get better and, presumably be less white, but unfortunately, "There is not yet a permanent cure."

> (...) Moss is speaking from a position of authority. His words will be heard in many circles. In calling "whiteness" an affliction, Moss is saying that an entire race suffers from an illness which it cannot control.[4]

Is it a physical illness? A mental illness? Left "untreated" by his "psychological and social-historical interventions," Moss is strongly suggesting that Caucasians are simply not capable of rational, non-racist thoughts and actions.

---

4 Ibid.

These same hateful beliefs are promoted in business. Christopher Rufo wrote about the United Way's Critical Race Theory "Racial Equity 21-Day Challenge" sponsored by Bank of America, Lowe's, and Truist Financial, which claims that America is systemically and institutionally racist, encourages participants to "decolonize [their] mind[s]" and to get "woke at work," and urges white people to "cede power to people of color."[5]

Truist Financial Corporation, Lowe's and Bank of America served as "presenting sponsors and equity champions" for the challenge, while Ally Financial, Atrium Health, Duke Energy and McGuireWoods participated as "equity ally sponsors." Ernst & Young, First National Bank, Gambrell Foundation, Grant Thornton and Knight Foundation joined the effort as "equity partner sponsors."[6]

Statements about the challenge include: "Racism is used to justify the position of the dominant group, White people in this case, and to uphold white supremacy and superiority. Everyone can be biased, and engage in bigoted and belittling behavior that is intolerant of other perspectives. But racism is by definition a form of oppression exercised by the dominant racial group (Whites)."[7]

Today, sadly, we are witnessing white hatred being promoted as an antidote to "systemic racism," despite the fact that we know racism can lead to physical as well as mental illness that lasts generations, because we have witnessed it in the black community.

This is Revenge Racism.

People seek revenge when they feel they have been attacked and suffered some unjust loss or injury or are humiliated, especially if they are made to feel powerless, foolish, or ashamed. Revenge is part of honour-shame cultures around the world where one feels the need to "defend the honor" of themselves, their family, ancestors, or some other group with which

5 Christopher F. Rufo, "Bank of Amerika," *City Journal*, August 18, 2021.

6 Tyler O'Neil, "Bank of America, Lowe's sponsored CRT training urging Whites to 'cede power to people of color,'" *Fox News*, August 19, 2021.

7 Christopher F. Rufo, "Bank of Amerika," op. cit.

they identify. It is essential to claim the mantel of victim before seeking revenge. And that is the position of CRT, BLM and the Progressive Left ideology. The Judeo-Christian ethic moved the world beyond honour/shame, yet here we are, devolving.

Social psychologist Ian McKee of Adelaide University in Australia explains, "People who are more vengeful tend to be those who are motivated by power, by authority and by the desire for status."[8]

What happened to the belief of Shakespeare about our shared humanity? In his famous play, *The Merchant of Venice* (now probably consigned to the dust bin with other works by dead, white males), Shakespeare wrote about the Jews who were attacked for being Jewish. For being.

> I am a Jew. Hath not a Jew eyes? Hath not a Jew hands, organs, dimensions, senses, affections, passions; fed with the same food, hurt with the same weapons, subject to the same diseases, healed by the same means, warmed and cooled by the same winter and summer as a Christian is? If you prick us do we not bleed? If you tickle us do we not laugh? If you poison us do we not die? And if you wrong us shall we not revenge? If we are like you in the rest, we will resemble you in that. If a Jew wrong a Christian, what is his humility? Revenge. If a Christian wrong a Jew, what should his sufferance be by Christian example? Why, revenge. The villainy you teach me I will execute, and it shall go hard but I will better the instruction. (III. i. 49–61.)

Many of us are familiar with the Golden Rule: "Do unto others what you would have them do unto you." But the original version was penned by Rabbi Hillel, who wrote: "Do not do to others what is hateful to you." But that is exactly what is taking place in America today.

Our children of every race and colour are being exposed to child abuse. For far too long, black people were looked upon as "lesser than." They were judged by color, not competence.

---

8 Michael Price, "Revenge and the people who seek it," *American Psychological Association*, June 2009, Vol. 40, No. 6, p. 34.

Today, despite the fact that we know the immorality and the illegality of racism, we are being dragged back into another race war based on revenge. Children are being taught that to be white is to be evil. That is Revenge Racism and it comes from a place of hate. Racism and hate harm children of all races and colours. I thought we had learned that already.

Imagine a young girl about eight years old who loves school. She has blond wavy hair that frames her oval face and has beautiful hazel eyes. She would be described as Caucasian: she has white skin. She couldn't wait to get up in the morning, get dressed, have breakfast and run for the school bus. When she came home, she couldn't wait to share her day with her mom.

One day, however, she came home from school very upset. She had been bullied. By her teachers.

"Mommy, why am I white? We learned today that white people are bad, oppressors and colonizers. We harm people of colour. And you and dad and Grandma and Grandpa and Nana and Papa did horrible things to black people. I'm so ashamed of being white."

She had learned in school that "white privilege is being able to navigate daily life in the American culture without having to think about race," and she was asked, "What does it mean for you to be white?" and told to, "Take a moment to talk with your neighbor about 'Whiteness.'" The teacher said, "Name some characteristics of white culture." But worst of all, she was basically told, "being white is a bad thing."[9]

And she ran to her room.

She came down late the next day.

She had painted her face brown.

This story is not far from the truth.

In October 2021, at a school board meeting, a Loudoun County, Virginia, mother said that she pulled her children from the public school system after her six-year-old daughter asked her if she was "born evil" because she is white.[10]

---

9 Ashe Schow, "Texas School District Shames White Students As Part Of 'Cultural Competence,' Parents Enraged," *Daily Wire*, April 27, 2021.

10 Emma Colton, "Loudoun County mom says 6-year-old asked her if she

Leaders in the Black Community are well aware of the effects of racism on mental and physical health. There are those in the Black community who maintain that the impact of centuries of unaddressed trauma still manifests today; it may even be inherited. Myrna Lashley, an assistant professor in the department of psychology at McGill University in Montreal, said: "Intergenerational trauma is trauma that is passed down. The pain and the angst and the hurt and the fear and...the sense of inferiority that has been imposed on you."[11]

The pain of racism is caused not only by one's lived experiences but also by the experiences of one's ancestors. These feelings are felt not only on an individual level but overall on a cultural level. Basically, being black in America means living with chronic post-traumatic stress disorder (PTSD) which includes a feeling of a foreshortened future, exaggerated startle responses, difficulty falling or staying asleep, outbursts of anger, and hypervigilance. These are signs of mental illness.

Dr. Joy DeGruy, a clinical psychologist with a doctorate in social work research and author of the book, *Post Traumatic Slave Syndrome: America's Legacy of Enduring Injury & Healing,* writes about how "... being Black in America impact(s) your stress level, therefore your body's ability to operate its own immune system."[12]

With all this lived experience, why are organizations like BLM and those which espouse Critical Race Theory, including teachers' unions, promoting white hatred? Why are we teaching white children to be ashamed of being white? Why are our children being taught that to be white is to be evil? Won't these teachings cause the same damage to white people as black people and in the end, damage our society itself?

And yet, we have a cultural theorist, author and Rutgers professor, Brittney Cooper, discussing the history of oppressive

---

was 'born evil' because she's White," *Fox News,* October 31, 2021.

11   Olivia Bowden, "Intergenerational trauma is 'pain' passed down generations, hurting Black people's health," *Global News,* June 22, 2020.

12   Jacquelyn Clemmons, "Trauma, but We Can Change That," *Healthline,* August 26, 2020.

power structures and the intersection of race and feminism. She gives her brief but spectacular take on "eloquent rage," sharing these thoughts on a panel entitled "Unpacking the Attacks on Critical Race Theory."[13] Ms. Cooper was also showcased on PBS in an interview with Judy Woodruff about her book, *Eloquent Rage: A Black Feminist Discovers Her Superpower.*[14]

Here are some of Cooper's comments from the Root Institute panel as recorded in *The Spectator*:

'I think that white people are committed to being villains in the aggregate.'

'I wouldn't be mad at the black people who want to get [white people] back.'

'[White people] are so corrupt. Their thinking is so morally and spiritually bankrupt about power that they fear viscerally, existentially about letting go of power.'

In response to a question about whether white people will ever give up power and resources, Cooper said, 'The thing I want to say to you is we gotta take these motherfuckers out,' before admitting, 'but we can't say that...I don't believe in a project of violence.'

'Whiteness is an inconvenient interruption' to black and indigenous people's existence.

When discussing children at the elementary school level, Cooper said, 'white kids are making assessments about their own racial superiority, or who's better than, or their own entitlement.'

'Despite what white people think of themselves, they do not defy the laws of eternity.'

---

13 Interview with Michael Harriot, "The Root Institute 2021: Unpacking the Attacks on Critical Race Theory," *The Root Institute*, September 21, 2021.

14 See the clip from the *PBS News Hour* here: https://www.pbs.org/newshour/brief/294191/brittney-cooper.

'White people's birth rates are going down...because they literally cannot afford to put newer generations into the middle class...we live in a system where even white people cannot sustain the cost of their own lives,' Cooper said, adding, 'it's super perverse, but also they kind of deserve it.'

'White life expectancy has gone down for the first time in the last couple years in a hundred years...when we look at whiteness in a total assessment, for all of the effort that they are putting in to dominate absolutely everything, the return on investment continues to diminish in every generation. And so that to me says we need to keep going.'[15]

This is Revenge Racism.

Did we learn nothing from the Nazi Party's obsession with race which focused on its perverted belief in the inferiority and superiority of the races? This opened the door for blaming various racial groups for all the problems facing the country. Have we forgotten the Rwanda genocide in 1994? Two tribes of people of similar color killing each other: "Neighbours killed neighbours and some husbands even killed their Tutsi wives, saying they would be killed if they refused. At the time, ID cards had people's ethnic group on them, so militias set up roadblocks where Tutsis were slaughtered, often with machetes which most Rwandans kept around the house. Thousands of Tutsi women were taken away and kept as sex slaves."[16]

The American left is claiming the root cause of virtually all problems facing the nation is "systemic racism" as theoretically instigated by one particular race.

This obsession with race led to what is now often referred to as "identity politics." Identity politics was a weapon in the arsenal of the Nazi Party. Using the national media, the Nazis divided the populace into specific identity groups and then promulgated grievance-riddled policies aimed at these manu-

---

15 Amber Athey, "Biden speaks at conference filled with anti-white, anti-police rhetoric," *The Spectator*, September 22, 2021.

16 See: "Rwanda genocide: 100 days of slaughter," *BBC*, April 4, 2019.

factured factions in order to foment anger at a specific identity group previously isolated by the party: the Jews. It appears today the media is aiding and abetting the Left in attacking people of no colour.

Remarkable, isn't it, the ease through which we descend into hate?

In 2015, the meta-analysis of Trusted Source found that racism is twice as likely to affect mental health than physical health, resulting in depression, stress, emotional distress, anxiety, post-traumatic stress disorder (PTSD), and suicidal thoughts.[17]

The American Academy of Pediatrics (AAP) also say that even if children do not directly experience racism themselves, they can be just as significantly affected by witnessing racism as those who experience it firsthand.[18]

"Racism is a threat to our children," states Dr. Nadine Burke Harris, a clinical psychologist for children and adolescents and the first Surgeon General of California. Racism—treating others negatively because of their skin colour or physical appearance—causes psychological trauma and toxic stress. This chronic activation of stress hormones leads to inflammation in the body and predisposes individuals to physical and mental health problems. Children who are exposed to demeaning experiences, including in school, may internalize the negative images and start believing they are how others sees them – dumb or bad or "less than."[19]

Claire McCarthy, MD, Senior Faculty Editor, Harvard Health Publishing, wrote: "Racism hurts children, in real and fundamental ways. It hurts not just their health, but their chanc-

---

17 Robert K. Hills, Ed., "Racism as a Determinant of Health: A Systematic Review and Meta-Analysis," NIH National Library of Medicine, September 23, 2015.

18 Maria Trent, et al., "The Impact of Racism on Child and Adolescent Health," American Academy of Pediatrics, *Pediatrics*, Volume 144, Issue 2, August 2019.

19 See: *A Guide to Toxic Stress*, Center on the Developing Child, Harvard University, https://developingchild.harvard.edu/guide/a-guide-to-toxic-stress/.

es for a good, successful life."[20] Despite our biological sameness, people continue to look for differences—and claim superiority.

Internalized negative stereotypes related to race can unconsciously erode self-perception and lead to chronic stress for children. Chronic stress leads to actual changes in hormones that cause inflammation in the body, a marker of chronic disease.

Children may also experience personally mediated racism early in their schooling, which may be internalized and ultimately affect their interactions with others. Early teacher-child interactions are important for long-term academic outcomes. The relationship of teacher to student across ages and grade levels influences school adjustment, literacy, math skills, grade point average, and scholastic aptitude test scores for the students.[21] When a teacher doesn't believe in you, you are less likely to believe in yourself.

Despite the facts about the dangers of racism, personally and culturally, Presdient Biden is pushing Critical Race Theory in US schools,[22] which includes a $5.3 million American History and Civics Education grant[23] for an attack on people of no colour. It would give priority for US history and civics grants to programs "that incorporate racially, ethnically, culturally and linguistically diverse perspectives" and specifically praises both Critical Race Theory and *The New York Times*' factually challenged "1619 Project."[24]

Boston University Professor Ibram X. Kendi approved by the Biden Administration for his anti-racism activism, pro-

20   Claire McCarthy, M.D., "How racism harms children," Harvard Health Publishing, January 8, 2020.

21   Maria Trent, et al., "The Impact of Racism on Child and Adolescent Health," op. cit.

22   Post Editorial Board, "Team Biden pushing Critical Race Theory in America's classrooms," *New York Post*, April 25, 2021.

23   Katabella Roberts and Jan Jekielek, "Biden's Proposed Funding of Critical Race Theory Puts US on a 'Very Dark Path': Inez Stepman," *The Epoch Times*, June 4, 2021.

24   Andrew Ujifusa, "Biden Administration Cites 1619 Project as Inspiration in History Grant Proposal," *Education Week*, April 19, 2021.

motes a new meaning to antiracism. As Christopher Caldwell explains:

> Anti-racists assume that the American system of politics, economics, and policing has been corrupted by racial prejudice, that such prejudice explains the entire difference in socioeconomic status between blacks and others, that the status quo must be fought and beaten, and that anyone not actively engaged in this system-changing work is a collaborator with racism, and therefore himself a legitimate target for attack.[25]

Kendi pushes the narrative that in order to undo past discrimination, we need to actively discriminate in favor of marginalized groups today. "The youngest of people are not colorblind—between three and six months, our toddlers are beginning to understand race and see race,"[26] said Kendi.

Really? It's all about race between three months and six months? For those of us who have children, we are well aware of our babies noticing differences. It is called "making strange," and it is normal. The baby becomes aware of his "tribe," the familiar people in his life. And when confronted by someone new, no matter race or creed, babies get anxious, nervous or upset and will often cling to their parents for reassurance. It's not about race. It's about "who are you to me?" But I digress.

CVS Health Corporation—the largest pharmacy chain in the United States—launched a mandatory "antiracist" training program for hourly employees to deconstruct their "privilege." During the program:

> Kendi who told 25,000 CVS employees that "to be born in [the United States] is to literally have racist ideas rain on our head consistently and constantly." Kendi argued that Americans are "walking through society completely

---

25 Christopher Caldwell, "Ibram X. Kendi, Prophet of Anti-racism," *National Review*, July 23, 2020.

26 Andrew Court, "Google staff are undergoing 'antiracism training," *Daily Mail*, September 9. 2021.

soaked in racist ideas," including children as young as two to three years old. "Our kids are basically functioning on racist ideas, choosing who to play with based on the kid's skin color," Kendi said. The solution, in part, is to "diagnose" employees as "racist" in order to help them become "antiracist" and "stop hurting somebody else."[27]

More assertions were made during the program for Google employees:

> Kendi suggested Americans be prescribed anti-racism and "respond in the same way that they respond when they are diagnosed with a serious illness." He reiterated that denial of racism is merely proof of it.
>
> "For me, the heartbeat of racism is denial and the sound of that denial is 'I'm not racist,'" he said.[28]

Seems Kendi writes from the victim's perspective. Someone please share with me how victimology has ever enhanced anyone's life.

In other words, the Biden administration is promoting Revenge Racism and mental illness. The "Proposed Priorities-American History and Civics Education" states:

> In turn, racially, ethnically, culturally, and linguistically responsive teaching and learning practices contribute to what has been called an "identity-safe" learning environment. According to the authors Dorothy Steele and Becki Cohn-Vargas, "Identity safe classrooms are those in which teachers strive to assure students that their social identities are an asset rather than a barrier to success in the classroom. And, through strong positive relationships and opportunities to learn, they feel they are welcomed, supported, and valued as members of the learning com-

---

27   Christopher F. Rufo, "True Privilege," *City Journal*, September 22, 2021.

28   Caroline Downey, "Google Launches Antiracism Program Teaching That America Is a 'System of White Supremacy,'" *National Review*, September 8, 2021.

munity.[29]

Identity safe? White children are being attacked for being white, taught that they are privileged oppressors, but the school is an identity safe space?

Biden's Department of Education has also linked to the Abolitionist Teaching Network's "Guide for Racial Justice & Abolitionist Social and Emotional Learning:"

> The Abolitionist Teaching Network Guide states "Abolitionist Teachers" should "[b]uild a school culture that engages in healing and advocacy. This requires a commitment to learning from students, families, and educators who disrupt Whiteness and other forms of oppression."[30]

Bettina Love, co-founder and chair of the board of the Abolitionist Teaching Network, said:

> "If you don't recognize that White supremacy is in everything we do, then we got a problem. I want us to be feared."[31]

So do bullies.

> Love conducted diversity training for managers and principals in September 2020. During this training, Love said schools didn't see Black people as humans and were anti-Black. Love also said schools "spirit murder" Black students.[32]

These "teachings" were shared in the Seattle Public School training session for teachers:

---

29 Department of Education, "Proposed Priorities-American History and Civics Education," *Federal Register*, April 19, 2021.

30 Ethan Barton, "Biden admin promotes radical group pushing critical race theory in schools," *Fox News*, July 21, 2021.

31 Ibid.

32 Ibid.

The United States is a "race-based white-supremist society," the training instructed, and white teachers must
"bankrupt [their] privilege in acknowledgement of [their]
thieved inheritance."

(...)

The central message is that white teachers must recognize
that they "are assigned considerable power and privilege
in our society" because of their "possession of white skin."
Consequently, to atone for their collective guilt, white
teachers must be willing to reject their "whiteness" and
become dedicated "anti-racist educator[s]."[33]

These teachers also discussed Bettina Love's concept of
"spirit murder," which states that American schools "murder
the souls of Black children every day through systemic, institutionalized, anti-Black, state-sanctioned violence." It is "a slow
death, a death of the spirit, a death that is built on racism and
intended to reduce, humiliate, and destroy people of color."[34]

This attack on people-of-no-color is no different than the
attacks on people of color over the centuries. The same people
who call themselves victims are victimizing non-colored people. This is a direct attack on the soul of America. A massive
"spirit murder."

President Donald Trump declared: "Teaching even one
child these divisive messages would verge on psychological
abuse. Indoctrinating generations of children with these extreme ideas is not just immoral—it is a program for national
suicide."[35]

The temptation to envy is a constant throughout history. We desire, said Shakespeare, "this man's art and that man's
scope."[36] Aeschylus said, "It is in the character of very few men

---

33 Christopher F. Rufo, "Teaching Hate," *City Journal*, December 18, 2020.

34 Bettina L. Love, "How Schools Are 'Spirit Murdering' Black and Brown
Students," *Education Week*, May 23, 2019.

35 Donald J, Trump, "A Plan to Get Divisive and Radical Theories Out of
Our Schools," *The Epoch Times*, June 23, 2021.

36 William Shakespeare, Sonnet 29: "When, in disgrace with fortune and
men's eyes," *Poetry Foundation*.

to honour without envy a friend who has prospered."[37] Goethe warned that although "hatred is active, and envy passive dislike; there is but one step from envy to hate."[38]

The Bible tells us: "'Revenge is mine,' says the Lord."

---

37 See: https://www.goodreads.com/quotes/298655-it-is-in-the-character-of-very-few-men-to.

38 See: https://www.brainyquote.com/quotes/johann_wolfgang_von_goeth_150549.

10

Bullying

Fear is such a powerful emotion for humans that when we allow it to take us over, it drives compassion right out of our hearts. — St. Thomas Aquinas

THE PROGRESSIVE LEFT, with their abusive, unrelenting bulling and promotion of cancel culture and revenge racism, is creating widespread mental unwellness in America. Cancel culture is actually teaching children how to bully, to attack those with whom they disagree to the point that a human being is emotionally destroyed. As Pamela Rutledge has written, "Cancel culture has turned into bullying with a cooler name. It promotes ostracization over education, condemnation over compassion, and is deaf to redemption and change."[1]

The bullying tactics of cancel culture scare people into submission out of fear of being punished. It is cyberbullying on steroids. Thanks to the ubiquity of social media, canceling someone has a broad reach and can do a lot of damage. "It is a very effective tool for wreaking psychological and social havoc when children are very vulnerable due to the normal developmental and healthy need to fit in, be liked, and have friends."[2]

---

1 Pamela B. Rutledge, "Cancel Culture: Accountability or Bullying?" *Psychology Today*, March 3, 2021.
2 Ibid.

Americans are being bullied into silence by Progressive Left-wing ideology that has transformed itself into a new religion, one might say cult, a term that doesn't refer to religion at all but is applied to a social movement that opposes critical thinking, the family unit and seeks truth by offering its followers a roadmap for their place in the universe while providing a moral code.[3] It is groupthink writ large.

As Friedrich Nietzsche observed, "In individuals, insanity is rare; but in groups, parties, nations and epochs, it is the rule."

Too many people have been bullied by Groupthink, a psychological phenomenon, and moral panic into seeing themselves as victims. We have all seen Groupthink in action, often found in cliques. Groupthink reduces one's courage to speak up against bullying. On the other hand, "[M]oral panics are often centered around people who are marginalized in society due to their race or ethnicity, class, sexuality, nationality, or religion. A moral panic often draws on known stereotypes and reinforces them. It can also exacerbate the real and perceived differences and divisions between groups of people."[4]

> The phrase "moral panic" and the development of the sociological concept is credited to the late South African sociologist Stanley Cohen (1942–2013). Cohen introduced the social theory of moral panic in his 1972 book titled, *Folk Devils and Moral Panics.*

He describes five stages.

> First, something or someone is perceived and defined as a threat to social norms and the interests of the community or society at large. Second, the news media and community members depict the threat in simplistic, symbolic ways that quickly become recognizable to the greater public. Third, widespread public concern is aroused by

---

3 See: Boze Herrington, "The Seven Signs That You're in a Cult," *The Atlantic*, June 18, 2014.

4 Ashley Crossman, "A Sociological Understanding of Moral Panic," *ThoughtCo.*, July 14, 2019.

the way news media portrays the symbolic representation of the threat. Fourth, the authorities and policymakers respond to the threat, be it real or perceived, with new laws or policies. In the final stage, the moral panic and the subsequent actions of those in power lead to social change in the community.[5]

One could consider the world's reaction to Covid 19 as moral panic.

Progressives are using moral panic to victimize black and indigenous people of colour, (BIPOC), portraying them as oppressed people with no free will, playing on a stereotype they themselves have created and employing Critical Race Theory as a means to achieve their desired social change.

Irving L. Janis, in his 1972 book, *Victims of Groupthink: A Psychological Study of Foreign-Policy Decisions and Fiascos*, defines "groupthink" as "a psychological drive for consensus at any cost that suppresses dissent and appraisal of alternatives in cohesive decision-making groups."[6] Furthermore, "[T}he suppression of individual opinions and creative thought can lead to poor decision-making and inefficient problem-solving."[7] Groupthink is a phenomenon in which the members prioritize unanimity over rational decision-making. Creativity and individuality are overshadowed by the desire to maintain the balance of the group and avoid disagreements.

Groupthink can take place under extreme stress or where moral dilemmas exist. Mass hysteria, an example of extreme Groupthink, can cause panic, or in some cases, manifest physical symptoms which have no medical basis.

> Groupthink can also refer to subtler processes of social or ideological conformity, such as participating in bullying or rationalizing a poor decision being made by one's

---

5　Ibid.

6　Cited by K. W. Grafton in "'Coronasteria' – Groupthink and the Psychology of Epidemic Hysteria," *National Newswatch*, May 25, 2020.

7　Lisa Fritscher, "How Mass Hysteria Is Related to Groupthink," *Very Well Mind*, July 24, 2020.

friends.[8]

Groups that prioritize their group identity and behave coldly toward "outsiders" may be more likely to fall victim to "groupthink which can have much worse consequences, leading groups to ignore ethics or morals, prioritize one specific goal while ignoring countless collateral consequences, or, at worst, instigate death and destruction."[9]

Groupthink can promote a culture of bullying, and all too often, people who would not typically bully another person will do it simply because "everyone does it, and they think they should get in on it also."[10] Groupthink, the assimilation to collectivist culture "is making us lose our capacity for empathy and for distinguishing between serious and unserious transgressions."[11] One could describe Groupthink as participating in tribalism.

Well-intentioned people are prone to making irrational decisions in the face of overwhelming pressure from the group, especially when the group lacks diversity. Look how many BIPOC looted and burned down cities following the death of George Floyd. Groupthink. Non-stop pressure on BIPOC to stand together to fight racism turned into riots. How many people who participated in those riots would never have done such a thing had they not been encouraged, "bullied," to participate and told over and over that they were victimized by the oppressors?

These incessant attacks on our words, our family structure and our values will lead to a society divided by a new malignant normality, even a malignant "morality." It will destroy the foundation of America, which for almost 246 years has promot-

---

8   "Groupthink," *Psychology Today,* https://www.psychologytoday.com/ca/basics/groupthink.

9   Ibid.

10   Cherie White, "Bullies, Groupthink and Fakery," *Chateau Cherie*, February 16, 2020.

11   Jon Ronson, TED talk, "When online shaming goes too far," https://www.ted.com/talks/jon_ronson_when_online_shaming_goes_too_far/transcript?language=en#t-823603.

ed life, liberty and the pursuit of happiness. If left unchecked, Progressive ideology will divide America into two tribes: the oppressors and the oppressed, obliterating one of the most important pillars in our ethic and the American Constitution: individual moral agency.

Tribalism existed long before the Judeo-Christian ethic came into being and remains today in countries where political freedom still does not exist.

Ayaan Hirsi Ali grew up in a tribal country—Somalia. She knows all too well the danger of tribalism. She wrote that tribalism leads to an almost blind hatred of a particular group and the use of deeply personal attacks on individuals to justify that hatred.

> There is also a blind commitment to one party (tribe) or the other where emotions are run high and there is a lack of trust in civic institutions.
> (...)
> The beautiful story of America, the reason so many people around the world still yearn to come here, is to a large extent founded on our rejection of tribalism and our establishment of civic, neutral institutions, based on the fundamental principle of equality before the law. These institutions are imperfect, of course, but they are far superior to the tribalism that rules other parts of the world. Our overcoming of such a natural urge is an accomplishment.
>
> As "woke" politics strengthens its grasp on our institutions — extending beyond the educational system into the media and now many corporations — that accomplishment is being eroded. The presumption of innocence, the commitment to blind justice and the whole notion of due process are all falling victim to spurious notions of "equity" and "anti-racism" — both of which carry within them an implicit intention to discriminate on racial lines.[12]

---

12   Ayaan Hirsi Ali, "Tribalism has come to the West," *UnHerd*, May 10, 2021.

Here we are in the twenty-first century, where information is ubiquitous and available to all, and yet we have allowed ourselves to be bullied into submission by a malignant morality and normality that is antithetical to Western culture. You know that feeling. You hear someone say something that you know makes no sense but stay quiet for fear of being demeaned, denigrated, and maligned on social media, which can even result in being canceled from your career. You know if you speak up you will be called a racist and nothing silences us today like the charge of being a racist.

We should all know the meaning of racist by now.

White people are bad people. They are oppressors and privileged. (Tell that to white families who have lost their meagre incomes because of the covid hysteria.) We can never listen to anything the oppressors may say. This attitude comes from Critical Race Theory. It has overtaken our concept of dignity of the person. And that dignity includes equality of respect. Somewhere along the way, we have moved away from a "freedom to" commitment to a "freedom from" commitment, including caring for others and respecting our elders.

It seems those who scream "racist!" have embraced race over compassion, personal rights over group responsibilities. They have themselves become oppressors, silencing the "other" because they have not been taught our shared stories, our shared humanity. That is a failure of our education system and a failure of government to teach the wonders of freedom and democracy.

This is also the result of teaching the pursuit of self—all about "me." And now we have added hatred of the "other" into our culture through Critical Race Theory and diversity politics—dividing us into multiple sub-groups based on race, colour, creed, and sexual orientation, pitting one group against another rather than uniting us as one people. We were once a nation held together by common shared stories, common values, common morals, a common language, and the teaching that all people are born with equal intrinsic value and all life is sacred.

Look how quickly we have been trained by Black Lives Matter to kneel in apology for our characteristics, not our character, violating everything bequeathed to us over the millennia.

Bullying is a type of social warfare, resulting in fear—fear of being shamed, shunned, or cut off from the group. Fear is the means by which all abusers, including bullies, disempower and control their victims. As Edmund Burke famously wrote: "No passion so effectively robs the mind of all its powers of acting and reasoning as fear."

God is weeping. He told us 365 times in the Hebrew Bible, "Do not fear." Three hundred and sixty-five times. One warning per day, every day. And what have we done? We have given into fear. What does fear do? Sometimes it gives us courage to fight back. Too often, fear frightens us unto submission. We allow ourselves of our own free will to become enslaved, again.

We, all of us, every race, colour, creed and sexual orientation were to have learned from the Jewish people's exile and slavery in Egypt that fear is contagious and holds us back. Instead of looking forward, as we are told to do, we look back, like Lot's wife.

After 400 years of enslavement under Pharaoh, the Jews were freed at last. And what did they do? Within days, they looked back fondly on the past. The food wasn't so bad. At least there were beds, shelter. There appears to be within us a desire to go back to the womb, back to the Garden where all of our needs are met—even if they are met under slavery. So, God, in His infinite wisdom and kindness, decided to wait until all of those forever enslaved to the past had died and the new generation, untouched by enslavement, would be ready to go forward, without fear, into the future.

It seems we need to be reminded over and over about freedom and its fragility. How easy it is to give it up—from fear of freedom itself. I remember the 1994 movie *The Shawshank Redemption*. We meet Andy Dufresne, who has been wrongly convicted of two murders and is sentenced to two consecutive life terms. In jail, he befriends Brooks, who has been in jail for decades. Brooks is paroled after serving fifty years. He leaves jail, his home for so long, the place where he was told what to do, when and how, and was given everything he needed. We watch him exit the gates and see right away that he is uncomfortable. He is taken into town, given a place to stay—and is lost. Frightened, he doesn't know what to do. He can't manage the freedom that was suddenly bestowed upon him, so he hangs himself.

That is what we are doing today, out of fear, we are hanging ourselves—slowly choking into submission, willing to give up our right to free speech, free assembly, free will—to freedom! And we sat back and watched as others, standing up for freedom and free speech, have been taken down, canceled for not accepting the new world view *Weltanschauung*—for having the audacity to share a different perspective than the one promoted by social media influencers and left-wing Progressives.

It is natural to feel fearful when a bully is undermining and disempowering you by cutting away at your self-confidence and self-esteem. Constant trivial nitpicking criticism sows the seeds of self-doubt, which eventually take root and sprout into full-blown fear. In addition, bullies co-opt others into isolating you, bad-mouthing you, ignoring you and distancing themselves from you.

While American values are under attack from the bullies of the left, Black and Indigenous People of Color (BIPOC) are being bullied as well, but from a different perspective. They, too, are being bullied by Black Lives Matter and Critical Race Theory. They are being told over and over to accept the designation of victim to the point where they give up their moral agency over time and submit to Groupthink. Groupthink fuels bullying, coercion to conform, us-versus-them thinking, strong efforts to stifle individuality, and social and emotional consequences if conformity is not achieved.

Bullying can damage the morals and values instilled in us by family and can lead to mental illness that lasts a lifetime.

Or is this a question of the chicken and the egg? Is it possible that mass mental illness has led to the ideology of the Progressive Left?

11

Industrialized Bullying

PROGRESSIVE LEFT-WING ideologues learned well from their success with "homophobia" and "Islamophobia" how to silence dissenting opinions and views. Bullies want to scare you and to define you, tell you who you are, often before you even know yourself. They want to describe you before you get a chance to become you. Like negative political ads—attack, attack, attack. Black Lives Matter and Critical Race Theory are employed to bully people into submission and silence, aided and abetted by mainstream media, social media and left wing politicians: the Progressives.

It was Marshall McLuhan who wrote, *The Medium is the Message*. I'd love to hear what he would say today about the easy abuse of and by social media. McLuhan wrote in 1967 that we live in a complex system of information, physically, physiologically, nervously, humanly. McLuhan also warned us about the need to pay attention to changes brought about by technology, the good and the bad, extensions and amputations. He wrote about how the telephone extends the voice, but also amputates the art of penmanship gained through regular correspondence.[1] I think it's safe to say that social media was also the beginning of an amputation in person-to-person interaction which allows the brain to pick up the minutiae of signals that enable us to

---

1 See *inter alia*: Marshall McLuhan, *Understanding Media: The Extensions of Man*, McGraw-Hill, 1964.

"read" others.

The Internet is the most revolutionary thing to happen to publishing since the invention of the Gutenberg printing press. For all the good social media was meant to achieve by extension, opening the discourse to many who would never have been heard, it released unintended consequences by encouraging anonymity and grandiose infantile delusions of entitlement to say anything. Anonymity makes it possible for people to express feeling-based opinion that is often 100 percent fact-free and rarely resembles anything close to truth. There is no accountability when one can espouse beliefs behind screen names. And, it opens a very wide door to abusive, anonymous bullying.

Anonymous comments, "the new norm" on social media, have serious social implications. They can inflame a situation, feeding the baser emotions of readers and listeners. Anonymity makes it possible to taunt others, to agitate, to provoke, but not to educate, making room for a meanness that has insinuated itself into everyday communication. This meanness promotes anger, the type of anger that, in its vehemence, can lead us away from compassion and empathy. It is acceptable, today, to speak rudely, disrespectfully, and thoughtlessly throughout the public square and to do irreparable damage to others in the process.

These unthinking words remain in the public discourse for perpetuity. There are no MRIs to detect broken souls, the result of language abused. In the long history of human development, civility is nascent. The past century has shown us the ease with which the foundation of civility is breached; it is still a tenuous veneer.

Civility is a firewall meant to keep us from reverting to our petty, selfish, ugly natural selves, and from expressing dangerous, hateful dogma. In the 1920s, Freud wrote that without some form of self-control, religious or otherwise, mayhem would rule as we fall to the lowest common denominator. Most recent studies from Yale University point to an innate lack of compassion from birth towards those who are different.[2] Anything that

---

2 CBS News: "Born good? Babies help unlock the origins of morality," *60*

takes the restraints away from civilization is welcomed by those who attack others whom they view as different or most often as weak, easy targets. Orwell's *Animal Farm* online. The ordeal of civility is an ordeal for a reason.

Continuous impersonal communication prevents the development of civilized, emotionally well-developed, compassionate citizens capable of rational, respectful dialogue. We allow this at the expense of the health of our children and the health of our community. We can't put the genie back in the bottle. But we must find ways to teach civility again, or we all lose.

Bullying Children and Mental illness

Many have fallen by the edge of the sword, but many more have fallen by the tongue. Blessed is one who has been sheltered from it, and has not experienced its fury.
—Ecclesiasticus 28:18-19

There is a tale about gossip and how it spreads.

A father says to his child, "Cut open that feather pillow and shake it into the wind."

The child does. And the feathers fly away wherever the wind takes them.

Then the father says: "Now go and find all the feathers!"

Needless to say, the children are baffled. How will they find all of the feathers?

Gossip is evil speech. Speech is meant to hold society together, but evil speech, gossip, destroys, because it undermines trust. It makes people suspicious about one another. It weakens the bonds that hold the group together. If unchecked, gossip will destroy any group it attacks: a family, a team, a community, even a nation. Malicious gossip undermines relationships, erodes the social bond, and damages trust.[3]

Minutes, July 28, 2013.

3 See: Rabbi Jonathan Sacks, "The Power of Shame," https://www.rabbi-sacks.org/covenant-conversation/metzora/the-power-of-shame%20Gossip/.

Gossip, especially today, is used to bully, destroy, cancel and silence anyone with an opinion that is not deemed politically correct, or "woke," by the elites of the time. Once shared, it can never be removed from the public square.

Today's bullies are the Progressives and their disciples of fear; people and institutions that attack your sense of self, attack you for your freedom of speech, freedom of thought, wear you down until apathy takes over—defeated by bullies. Fear can be used as a tool to manipulate others. People in positions of power, past and present, have effectively used fear to control certain aspects of society. "When one is gripped by fear of a threat, real or imagined, their rational and higher cognitive capacities shut down, making them easily manipulable by anyone that promises safety from the threat."[4]

"No passion so effectually robs the mind of all its powers of acting and reasoning as fear," wrote the eighteenth-century philosopher Edmund Burke. And fear leads to submission.

Progressive teachings are contributing to discrimination as described by Ronald E. Riggio:

> The roots of discrimination and prejudice involve psychological processes, such as in-group/out-group biases (the "we-they" feeling), and social dominance, where one group (the in-group) is considered superior to outgroup members.[5]

This is exactly what is taking place in our schools as a result of including Critical Race Theory in the curricula.

Left-wing progressivism uses gossip and bullying to take over. Bullying may even be thought of as a type of fascism. Bandy X. Lee asserts, "[F]ascism is not an ideology or political strategy but a societal pathology."[6] It is social warfare. Fascism

4 See: "Fear and Social Control" video and transcript, *Academy of Ideas,* https://academyofideas.com/2015/11/fear-and-social-control/.

5 Ronald E. Riggio, "Religious Bullying in Schools: Bullying in the Name of God," *Psychology Today,* August 28, 2012.

6 Bandy X. Lee, "Mental Health Experts Warn of a Malignant Normality," *Psychology Today,* May 29, 2018.

and bullying promote fear, and with enough fear, people are silenced into submission, giving up their freedom. As Don Carroll explains, "Freedom is extremely important for good mental health. Good mental health is characterized by having personal freedom—to be free to make good choices for one's self and others."[7]

From grade school to university, our children are being shamed and psychologically abused. Never assume the bullying will end without intervention, nor should you expect that your child will get over it or be fine. As Rosiland S. Dorlen explains:

> Bullying can contribute to students feeling socially isolated, worthless or depressed. In addition, the psychological effects of bullying can last well into adulthood and increase a person's chance of experiencing things like anxiety disorders.[8]

Bullying leads to long-term mental health issues, including suicide.

Young people are being shamed by a steady media diet of toxic cultural messages. Their core identities are under attack.[9] And isn't that what Progressives desire? People of no colour to be ashamed of themselves? Shame is so powerful that it can impact the whole trajectory of a person's life.

Shame is connected to the intensely painful experience of believing that we are flawed and unworthy of love, acceptance and belonging. People who feel shame feel worthless, embarrassed, humiliated, and unclean. These feelings often lead to fear, blame, disconnection and isolation. Shame can be a contributing factor in depression, anxiety, and low self-esteem.[10]

When we witness someone else being bullied and we do

---

7 Don Carroll, "Freedom and Mental Health," *North Carolina Lawyers Assistance Program*, April 8, 2014.

8 Rosiland S. Dorlen, "Bullying," *Find a Psychologist*, undated.

9 See: Karen L. Pace, "Shame is often at the heart of bullying," *Michigan State University Extension*, September 17, 2012.

10 See: "5 Ways Shame Can Shape Your Life," *Clearview Treatment Programs*, undated.

nothing, we may feel shame. Shame often leads to feelings of fear and insecurity which present barriers to responding from our core values and beliefs. We may also begin to believe the messages that say we are "less than" because of a difference we have. When we unconsciously feel shame, we may respond by shutting down, acting out, or attacking others—revenge. I wonder how many people have taken to violence because of shame instilled in them.

When the bullying is physical, most parents do not hesitate to report incidents. But, when the bullying is emotional or verbal, parents are not sure what to do. They fear to make things worse for their child. While this concern is, sadly, valid, it is never a good idea to ignore bullying.[11]

Remember the saying, "Sticks and stones can break my bones but names will never hurt me?" I don't know why this was ever shared and so broadly. The truth is that I'd be rather be attacked by sticks and stones than be attacked by words that are expressly meant to demean me, denigrate me, shame me, belittle me. You cannot see a broken soul or a broken heart, a broken will, and share it with others.

Bullies know that.

What will happen when children are bullied by teachers at school and adults are bullied for not accepting progressivism as their religion? What will our mental health be like?

And what about the bullies themselves? They behave as though the emotional and physical health of their victims is not important or is at least less important than their own desire for the thrill of aggression and dominance. They use others as objects for their own ends. People who see themselves as objects can easily become victims, because they lose sight of their free will, their moral agency; or perhaps they were never taught that they are the subjects of their destiny and not born into their fate. Furthermore, bullies are not compensating for low self-esteem as once thought:

---

11 Sherri Gordon, "How to Respond to a Teacher Who Bullies," *VeryWell Family,* July 18, 2020.

> [N]ew research shows that most bullies have excellent self-esteem. Bullies usually have a sense of entitlement and superiority over others, and lack compassion, impulse control and social skills.[12]

How sad is this? We know that bullies are bad, yet we are validating them. The ninth commandment revealed at Mount Sinai 3500 year ago says: *Thou shall not bear false witness.* You won't lie. You won't gossip. You won't bully. Words abused are weapons of destruction.

Social media has changed bullying. It no longer stays within a small community. Gossip, name calling and lying are spread in a blink of an eye through social networking, even breaking the sanctity of our homes. I cannot say this enough: Language is a powerful weapon. It is easier to recover from a broken bone than a broken soul. Children do not commit suicide over broken bones.

> According to statistics reported by ABC News, nearly 30 percent of students are either bullies or victims of bullying, and 160,000 kids stay home from school every day because of fear of bullying.[13]

Bullying at any age can be devastating, especially when there are millions of people with mental illness on line. Once diagnosed with a mental illness, one lives with it forever. Where is the concern for safe spaces for those who carry on with that mental illness? Sadly:

> Suicide continues to be one of the leading causes of death among children under the age of 14. Many studies show that being bullied can cause mental illness in children. Bully victims are between 2 to 9 times more likely to consider suicide than non-victims, according to studies by Yale University. Suicide is the third leading cause of death among young people, resulting in about 4,400 deaths per

---

12 See: "The Psychology Of Bullying," *Theravive*, undated.

13 "Bullying and Suicide," *Bullying Statistics*, undated.

year, according to the CDC. For every suicide among young people, there are at least 100 suicide attempts. At least half of suicides among young people are related to bullying. Ten to 14 year old girls may be at even higher risk for suicide. More than 14 percent of high school students have considered suicide, and almost 7 percent have attempted it.[14]

A study done in Britain in 2009 found that children who get bullied are often less confident and more emotional than their peers who aren't victimized. Researchers found a relationship between bullying and psychotic symptoms: 'The greater the severity of bullying, the stronger the link – suggests that bullying actually helped cause children's psychotic symptoms, rather than vice-versa."[15]

There is another "side-effect" to bullying that does not often get discussed—nonsuicidal self-injury—cutting. Nonsuicidal self-injury, often simply called self-injury, is the act of deliberately harming one's own body, such as cutting or burning oneself. It's usually not meant as a suicide attempt. Rather, this type of self-injury is a way to cope with emotional pain, intense anger and frustration.

> Maltreatment and victimization during childhood and adolescence may be a key factor associated with self-stigma. Self-stigma takes place when individuals internalize the negative public attitudes and stereotypes about their status and further experience a wide range of adverse costs related to these prejudices. Thus, self-stigma evokes intense feelings of embarrassment, worthlessness, and self-blame influencing one's self-esteem. Decreased self-esteem, associated with self-stigma, has been associated with both deliberate self-harm and depressive symptoms.[16]

---

14 Ibid.

15 Reuters Health, "Bullying victims have more psychotic symptoms," Reuters, May 4, 2009.

16 Maria N. K. Karanikola, Anne Lyberg, Anne-Lise Holm, and Elisabeth Severinsson, "The Association between Deliberate Self-Harm and School

Amanda Todd

Amanda Todd was a 15-year-old Canadian student and victim of cyberbullying who hanged herself at her home in Port Coquitlam, British Columbia. The bullying had led her to become a cutter. She cried all the time. She admitted to self-medicating with drugs and alcohol. She had previously attempted suicide.

She killed herself in 2012. Here we are 10 years later. We still witness children taking their lives from being bullied.

One report found that 64% of students who were bullied never told anyone about it. Even when injuries occurred, 40% of bullied students still never reported the incident. Often, kids feel like reporting a bully won't do any good. Not only do they feel powerless, but they also worry that the bully will only make their lives worse if they speak up. In fact, 40% of kids who are bullied report that the people who targeted them were bigger and physically stronger, while 56% report that those bullying them had the ability to influence other students' perceptions of them.[17]

Amanda's last calls for help were silent. A month before her suicide, she shared a nine-minute video on YouTube, which contains themes of self-harm, cyberbullying and suicide. She used flash cards in the video instead of her voice—because she no longer believed she had one.

Many bullied children suffer in silence. They learn to be silent. Will the children being bullied today by teachers learn to be silent and submit?

Toronto Star reporter Victoria Ptashnick asked in an article about witnessing bullying like what had happened to Amanda: "Why did I, a nice kid by all other accounts, stay silent and do nothing…Why did the kids who watched Todd's bullying do

Bullying Victimization and the Mediating Effect of Depressive Symptoms and Self-Stigma: A Systematic Review," *National Library of Medicine*, October 11, 2018.

17 See: Sherri Gordon, "Why Victims of Bullying Often Suffer in Silence," *Very Well Family,* December 5, 2021.

the same?"[18] We lose sight of the fact that the evil of selfishness is insidious. It exists on a continuum, and if we don't pay attention, we slide, individually and collectively, into evil, selfish actions like silence. I would like to suggest that the greatest evil is committed by sins of omission, *ignorantia affectata*, a cultivated ignorance, a wilful lack of knowledge. As Ms. Ptashnick confessed, "I simply watched. I now realize that made me equally responsible in the act."[19]

Too many of us have come to accept uncivilized, hurtful, demeaning behaviour in our institutions; schools, parliaments, and in the media; television and internet. According to Dieter Wolke and Suzet Tanya Lereya:

> Children who were victims of bullying have been consistently found to be at higher risk for common somatic problems such as colds, or psychosomatic problems such as headaches, stomach aches or sleeping problems, and are more likely to take up smoking. Victims have also been reported to more often develop internalising problems and anxiety disorder or depression disorder.
> (...)
> Children who were victims of bullying have been consistently found to be at higher risk for internalizing problems, in particular diagnoses of anxiety disorder and depression in young adulthood and middle adulthood (18–50 years of age).Furthermore, victims were at increased risk for displaying psychotic experiences at age 18 and having suicidal ideation, attempts and completed suicides.[20]

According to a study from American Academy of Pediatrics and reported in *Science Daily*:

> Cyberbullying — the use of the Internet, phones or other

---

18 Victoria Ptashnick, "Bullying: Bystanders must take some responsibility, reporter says," *Toronto Star*, October 19, 2012.

19 Ibid.

20 Dieter Wolke and Suzet Tanya Lereya. "Long-term effects of bullying," *National Library of Medicine*, February 10, 2015.

technologies to repeatedly harass or mistreat peers — is often linked with teen suicide in media reports. However, research presented Oct. 20, 2012 at the American Academy of Pediatrics (AAP) National Conference and Exhibition in New Orleans, showed that the reality is more complex. Most teen suicide victims are bullied both online and in school, and many suicide victims also suffer from depression.

From the abstract, "Cyberbullying and Suicide: A Retrospective Analysis of 41 Cases," researchers searched the Internet for reports of youth suicides where cyberbullying was a reported factor. Information about demographics and the event itself were then collected through searches of online news media and social networks. Finally, descriptive statistics were used to assess the rate of pre-existing mental illness, the co-occurrence of other forms of bullying, and the characteristics of the electronic media associated with each suicide case.

The study identified 41 suicide cases (24 female, 17 male, ages 13 to 18) from the U.S., Canada, the United Kingdom and Australia. In the study, 24 percent of teens were the victims of homophobic bullying, including the 12 percent of teens identified as homosexual and another 12 percent of teens who were identified as heterosexual or of unknown sexual preference.

Suicides most frequently occurred in September (15 percent) and January (12 percent) although these higher rates may have occurred by chance. The incidence of reported suicide cases increased over time, with 56 percent occurring from 2003 to 2010, compared to 44 percent from January 2011 through April 2012.

Seventy-eight percent of adolescents who committed suicide were bullied both at school and online, and only 17 percent were targeted online only. A mood disorder was reported in 32 percent of the teens, and depression symptoms in an additional 15 percent.

"Cyberbullying is a factor in some suicides, but almost always there are other factors such as mental illness or face-to-face bullying," said study author John C. LeBlanc, MD, MSc, FRCPC, FAAP. "Cyberbullying usually occurs in the context of regular bullying."

Cyberbullying occurred through various media, with Formspring and Facebook specifically mentioned in 21 cases. Text or video messaging was noted in 14 cases.

"Certain social media, by virtue of allowing anonymity, may encourage cyberbullying," said Dr. LeBlanc. "It is difficult to prove a cause and effect relationship, but I believe there is little justification for anonymity."[21]

These statistics are from 2012. It is now 2022. Imagine.

Bullied By Adults: Nicolas Sandmann's Story

We talk to kids in school about bullying on social media, especially now that bullying has moved from the school yard right into the homes of our children through social media. But how do we protect our children from media bullying on the nightly news? It seems we don't, out of fear of being canceled or bullied, or shamed ourselves by the ever-growing infiltration of Progressive values. The Covington Boys are the prime example of the failure to protect. At the same time, they are an extraordinary example of fighting back, refusing to be silenced. These Kentucky students were at the March for Life in Washington, D.C., January 19, 2019 (that, I am sure, was enough for the vultures to go after them), when a video was taken and disseminated that showed the boys in a dark light. This led to a nationwide media frenzy, and the boys were falsely accused of mocking a Native American, prompting hundreds of threats against the school and the school's students from across the country by

---

21 "Cyberbullying only rarely the sole factor identified in teen suicides," *Science Daily*, October 20, 2012.

phone, email, and social media. Condemnation also came from Covington Catholic High School, the Diocese of Covington, and even March for Life President Jeanne Mancin.

But for me, the number one failure goes to the bishop of their diocese, who attacked his own students without asking them what happened or viewing the evidence. He left them hanging. He joined the chorus of hateful #PCGroupThink. That he chose not to trust his students means he did not trust that his school had instilled proper morals and values in his students.

The only adult in the room was 16-year-old Nick Sandmann, the Covington Catholic High School junior who said: "We're a Catholic school and it's not tolerated. They don't tolerate racism, and none of my classmates are racist people."[22]

It wasn't until late January 25, amidst mounting pressure, that Bishop Roger Foys issued a new statement admitting that the Diocese "should not have allowed ourselves to be bullied and pressured into making a statement prematurely, and we take full responsibility for it" and "especially apologiz[ing] to Nicholas Sandmann and his family as well as to all CovCath families who have felt abandoned during this ordeal."[23]

He had allowed himself to be bullied? He was bullied? He is the adult in the room. He is a Catholic bishop. And he threw his students, his wards, his children under a bus. And I cannot ever forgive that. A Catholic bishop represents God to his flock. Our children need to know that those closest to them will protect them. And in this atmosphere of #PCGroupThink, and identity politics, and feeling based everything, they need our protection more than ever before.

These students were exemplary in their behaviour when faced with a Native American, and I mean *faced*, along with a group of nasty, hateful black people from an obscure "religious" organization who spewed hateful comments. How did we get to a place where we believe a Native American and black peo-

22 Eun Kyung Kim, "Nick Sandmann on encounter with Nathan Phillips: 'I wish I would've walked away'," *Today*, January 23, 2019.

23 Dennis Romero, "Bishop apologizes to teen who faced off with Native American," *NBC News*, January 25, 2019.

ple just for being Native or black? Is that not the definition of racism? Is that not what happened for decades in America—a white person was believed over a black person merely for being white!

Yet, nothing was going to stop media personalities like *Today's* Savannah Guthrie, another adult very adept at bullying children. She had the audacity to ask on January 23, when the truth had been exposed, whether Sandmann felt he owed anyone an apology or had assumed fault for the clash. WHAT?

And then she asked Sandmann about the expression he wore on his face as he faced off against Phillips. Some have characterized the look as a smirk, but Sandmann describes it differently:

> I see it as a smile, saying that this is the best you're going to get out of me. You won't get any further reaction of aggression. And I'm willing to stand here as long as you want to hit this drum in my face.[24]

Sandmann said it was unfair to have his character weighed up by one look:

> People have judged me based off one expression, which I wasn't smirking, but people have assumed that's what I have," he said. "And they've gone from there to titling me and labeling me as a racist person, someone that's disrespectful to adults, which they've had to assume so many things to get there without consulting anyone that can give them the opposite story.[25]

So here we have a media personality acting like a bully on TV. Bullying a 16-year-old.

This qualifies as journalism? Assume guilt if the person is white, male (and heaven forbid!), wearing a MAGA hat. Jump on that "story" without checking facts. Journalists on the left are

---

24 See: Elisha Fieldstadt, "Covington Catholic student in D.C. march video explains 'smirking' at Native American activist," *NBC News*, January 23, 2019.

25 Ibid.

the new leaders of the social justice movement.

If he had not been wearing the MAGA hat, would NBC have cared? Would anyone else in MSM or social media have cared? No.

Nicolas Sandmann was not bullied by his peers. He was bullied by journalists—adults who intentionally and repeatedly caused him discomfort and emotional abuse. These influential adults believed that the ends justified the means. Attacking a white student as a possible white supremacist to promote the idea that America is systemically racist.

They should be fired as an example. No adult journalist should ever feel that they can attack a child over a story, ever.

In America, all 50 states have some kind of anti-bullying law, and schools are increasingly being called upon to implement bullying prevention programs. Perhaps we need to provide sensitivity training to these social justice journalists too.

Shame on all of them. From the bishop, in particular, to the so-called adults covering that story.

The attorneys representing Covington Catholic High School student Nicholas Sandmann and his family have put more than 50 media entities on notice that their false reporting has put them in serious legal jeopardy. The list includes 50-plus names of organizations or individuals: from presidential hopeful Elizabeth Warren to actress Alyssa Milano; individual journalists including Maggie Haberman, Ana Cabrera and David Brooks; national media outlets like the *The New York Times, CNN, GQ* and *TMZ*; and the dioceses of Covington and Lexington as well as the archdioceses of Louisville and Baltimore.

As a mother and grandmother, I am appalled. Look how far we have fallen. From being bullied by one's principal to being bullied on line to being bullied in mainstream media. I have nothing but admiration and compassion for Mr. Sandmann and his family and friends, and now their lawyers. *CNN, The Washington Post* and *NBC Universal* were sued and Sandmann won.[26]

---

26 Lauren Artino, "CNN settles lawsuit with Nick Sandmann," *Fox News*, January 7, 2020.

The effects of bullying on bystanders

New research suggests students who watch as their peers endure the verbal or physical abuses of another student could become as psychologically distressed, if not more so, by the events than the victims themselves.[27] Bystanders who do nothing inadvertently give bullies permission to go on being bullies.

Throughout history, we have witnessed political leaders make executive orders that take power away from some people, and the rest of the citizenry, out of fear, remain silent, giving them their silent permission. Bullies and bystanders may also be more likely to take drugs and drink alcohol, according to the findings, which are reported in the *School Psychology Quarterly*. Students who witnessed acts of bullying were more likely to report greater psychological distress than those students who were bullies or victims. This was the case even for students who had not been victims themselves, although being both a witness and a victim did also significantly predict mental health problems.

Dr. Ian Rivers, the study's lead author, wrote:

It's well documented that children and adolescents who are exposed to violence within their families or outside of school are at a greater risk for mental health problems than those children who are not exposed to any violence. It should not be a surprise that violence at school will pose the same kind of risk. It is possible that those students who had been victimized at different times may be experiencing it all over again psychologically. Meanwhile, those who are witnesses may worry that they, too, will be the bully's target sometime in the future and that causes great distress and anxiety.[28]

Previous research has also shown that students who wit-

---

27 See: Ian Rivers, V. Paul Poteat, Nathalie Noret, Nigel Ashurst, "Observing Bullying at School: The Mental Health Implications of Witness Status," *School Psychology Quarterly*, Vol. 24, No. 4.

28 Ibid.

ness acts of bullying, but are not directly involved, feel guilty for not interceding on the victim's behalf, which may help explain the higher levels of mental distress.

Look around. How many social media posts have you seen describing an attack in a subway, for example, and no-one helps? They are either watching, studiously ignoring, or filming on their phones.

Victimization and bystander behavior were found to be directly and negatively associated with emotion regulation. Marina Camodeca and Elena Nava suggest that being involved directly (as victim) or indirectly (as bystander) in bullying at school is associated with difficulties in emotional wellbeing in adulthood. Furthermore, it reveals that behavioral and physiological indexes associated with emotion regulation dissociate, suggesting that subtle physiological changes may remain hidden from explicit behavior.[29]

Bystanders who aren't on the receiving end also suffer, because watching bullying causes vicarious trauma. Is it possible that witnessing this bullying can lead to a contagion of fear, which can lead to submission? Recent research found that witnessing workplace bullying is associated with an increased risk of developing depressive symptoms over the subsequent 18 months.[30] Is there a difference between being an adult bullied in the workplace, or being bullied in school, or in the public square?

Sherri Gordon writes, "Many times, kids feel like they need to accept occasional bullying in order to belong. As a result, they will succumb to peer pressure and accept bullying as a way to maintain their social standing. This mixture of peer pressure and bullying often exists in cliques."[31] Sound famil-

---

29 Marina Camodeca and Elena Nava, "The Long-Term Effects of Bullying, Victimization, and Bystander Behavior on Emotion Regulation and Its Physiological Correlates," *Journal of Interpersonal Violence,* Vol 37, Issue 3-4, June 2022.

30 Stacey Colino, "The Long Reach of Adult Bullying," *US News & World Report, Health,* December 15, 2017.

31 Sherri Gordon, "Why Victims of Bullying Often Suffer in Silence," *Very Well Family,* December 5, 2021.

iar? I remember this as quite common as a student, but now? How many adults have felt the pressure of peers? How many have been pressured by peers to remain silent for fear of being canceled, or losing their jobs? How many have remained silent in restaurants as bullies verbally abused them or others?

When it comes to protecting children at school, educators must ensure an environment where reporting bullying is not only acceptable but expected. This also means that they need to be careful about how they handle reports of bullying including how they interact with students who report being harassed and mistreated. How sad is it that we need to ensure that same safe environment in the public square before is it too late?

What are the long term effects of bullying?

Every victim of bullying will have a different answer, but the result is the same. The effects of bullying are long-lasting and do not disappear in the adult years.[32] Bullying is an attempt to instill fear and self-loathing. Bullying attacks one's self-esteem. It is easier to mold someone with low self-esteem than someone who has self-confidence; hence, industrialized bullying in our culture. According to the website, *Mental Help:*

> Being bullied teaches you that you are undesirable, that you are not safe in the world, and (when it is dished out by forces that are physically superior to yourself) that you are relatively powerless to defend yourself. When you are forced, again and again, to contemplate your relative lack of control over the bullying process, you are being set up for Learned Helplessness (e.g., where you come to believe that you can't do anything to change your ugly situation even if that isn't true), which in turn sets you up for hope-lessness and depression.
>
> (…)
>
> Much of what passes for identity in the young (and in the older too) is actually a kind of other-confidence, which

---

32 See: "What Are The Effects Of Bullying On Your Adult Years?," *Our Family World*, May 31, 2015.

is to say that many people's self-confidence is continual-
ly shored up by those around them telling them in both
overt and subtle ways that they are good, worthy people.
This is one of the reasons people like to belong to groups
– it helps them to feel good about themselves. Bullying
teaches people that they are explicitly not part of groups;
that they are outcasts and outsiders.

(...)

In the short term: anger, depression, anxious avoidance of
settings in which bullying may occur, greater incidence of
illness, lower grades than non-bullied peers, and suicidal thoughts and feelings may occur. (In one British retrospective bullying experiences survey, 20% of the sample attempted suicide secondary to having been bullied,
whereas only 3% of participants who were not bullied
attempted suicide.)

In the long term: reduced occupational opportunities;
lingering feelings of anger and bitterness; desire for revenge; difficulty trusting people; interpersonal difficulties,
including fear and avoidance of new social situations; the
increased tendency to be a loner; perception of self as easy
to victimize, overly sensitive, and thin-skinned; self-esteem problems (don't think well of self); and increased
incidence of continued bullying and victimization.[33]

This creates a perfect storm for power-hungry ideologues
who want to tear down the morals and values that underpin
America and at the same time develop a victim class: people of
colour.

Dieter Wolke and Suzet Tanya Lereya define bullying as
"the systematic abuse of power and is defined as aggressive behaviour or intentional harm-doing by peers that is carried out
repeatedly and involves an imbalance of power." And then there
is indirect bullying which is "characterised by social exclusion
(eg, you cannot play with us, you are not invited, etc.) and ru-
mour spreading."[34]

---

33 "The Long Term Effects of Bullying," *Mental Help*, undated.

34 Dieter Wolke and Suzet Tanya Lereya, "Long-term effects of bullying,"

Bullying takes place in abusive relationships. Bullies are often aggressive, intimidating and controlling of their intimate partners. Edmund Burke wrote: "The greater the power, the more dangerous the abuse," including patterns of physical, mental, and/or emotional abuse. Unless strong and effective boundaries are established, the bully is likely to repeat and intensify the abuse. Those who remain passive and compliant are more likely to be bullied. Preston Ni writes, "Many bullies are also cowards: When their victims begin to show backbone and stand up for their rights, a bully will often back down."[35]

There are lasting psychological effects on the victims and lasting effects on the bully as well. That is the reason parents need to speak up.

National Library of Medicine, February 10, 2015.

35 Preston Ni, "The 5 Major Ways Adults Bully Each Other," *Psychology Today*, January 22, 2017.

12

The Need to Develop Resilience

AMERICAN WRITER Paul Tough in his book, *How Children Succeed*, argues that children who do well have learned "persistence, self-control, curiosity, conscientiousness, grit, and self-confidence:"[1] Resilience.

Amanda Todd, like so many other children, did not have the resilience to fight bullying. Yet, Nicholas Sandmann was resilient.

We need to help our children develop resilience, but we also need to help adults overcome fear of bullying so they can fight back and protect the dignity of those they love. We need to teach flexibility to our children in their responses to something negative, help them see that there is a future beyond this current situation and stop focusing on the negative. Positive thinking enables your child to see the good things in life and keep going even during the most challenging situations and to avoid dwelling on the negative. The more children engage in victim-thinking, the worse off they are. We need to empower our sons and daughters to take control over their lives, to stand up for themselves, to speak up for themselves. Otherwise, we run the risk of turning them into victims, filled with a sense of helplessness, which I know from personal experience can lead to despair and depression.

---

1   Paul Tough, *How Children Succeed: Grit, Curiosity, and the Hidden Power of Character*, Houghton Mifflin Harcourt, 2012.

One of the worst things you can do to a young person is to convince them they're some kind of victim and that the world is against them. Yet, isn't that the result of Critical Race Theory's instilling in children of color the belief that they are perpetual victims? Instead, we should encourage them to try to discover what they can learn from the situation and how best to overcome bullying.[2] Bullying is not something that goes away on its own; never underestimate the power of bullying.

So why is it that some children are devastated by bullying, while others are not? Is there some personal characteristic or trait that buffers and protects them against internalizing the harm intended through bullying and cyberbullying?

The answer is a resounding "yes." That trait is "resilience" or the ability to "bounce back" and successfully adapt to stressful situations. According to the co-director of the Cyberbullying Research Center, Sameer Hinduja, "Resilient kids are those, who for a variety of reasons, are better able to withstand external pressures and setbacks and are less negatively impacted in their attitudes and actions than their less-equipped peers when facing this type of victimization."[3]

Remember, when you get bullied, know that you touched a nerve in the bully. While you think of yourself as weak, there is something strong about you that frightens the bully. Hold on to that.

It was found, though, that the more children were bullied, the less resilient they were. According to various researchers:

> [B]ully perpetrators were less committed to academic success, getting school work and homework completed, and following school rules. They found that lower levels of paternal care, higher levels of authoritarianism, and overprotectiveness were reported by perpetrators of bullying. Having low attachment to parents, school, and teachers, feeling less teacher support, and feeling alienated from

---

2 See Sherri Gordon, "10 Ways to Help Your Child Overcome Bullying," *Very Well Family*, May 28, 2021.

3 Cited in "Bullying: Why Kids Need to Learn Resilience," *PD Resources*, https://blog.pdresources.org/bullying-why-kids-need-to-learn-resilience/.

school may have been risk factors for bully perpetration. Student's perceptions of bully perpetrators and victims were examined... Students described perpetrators of bullying as those who wanted to show they were powerful, were envious of their victim, lacked respect for others, were seeking feelings of superiority, and to feel better about themselves.

(...)

Bullying has often been associated with anxiety. Anxiety has been experienced by many people and at various levels. Anxiety has been associated with victimization... Najafi et al. (2017) found that anxiety and victimization were directly related, and anxiety had a direct effect on suicidal thoughts with victimization as a mediator. Anxiety may have had a serious impact on those who suffered from it. Exposure to bullying during childhood was known to contribute to mental health problems such as anxiety.[4]

Think about that: anxiety and victimization were directly related. I can relate to that only too well. Looking back, being bullied by my principal probably started me on my road to anxiety that even today leads me down into the abyss of depression.

And here we are teaching children of color to BE victims.

Negative emotions can weigh heavily on people who believe they'll always be victims, building and festering when they aren't addressed. Over time, these feelings might contribute to angry outbursts, depression, isolation, and loneliness.

Personal attacks on one's character add nothing to the conversation but can do a great deal of damage to one's self-esteem. We need to accept that just as no one gives us self-esteem, no one can take it away. We develop self-esteem by doing, by succeeding. We lose self-esteem, not because someone takes it away, but because *we let it go*. We let bullies, many of them frightened little people, hiding behind screen names on-line to convince us that there's something wrong with us. Often, we

---

4 Suzette A. Bean, "Bullying and Resilience in Elementary School Children and Mitigating Pro-Social Behaviors," Walden University Dissertation. https://scholarworks.waldenu.edu/cgi/viewcontent.cgi?article=8157&context=dissertations.

end up giving away pieces of ourselves.

Do not give them the satisfaction. Remember no one can take away your "self." You can lose an arm or a leg, but the self remains whole.

13
Bullied from White Privilege

No one heals himself by wounding another.
—St. Ambrose

N OW, IN THE TWENTY-FIRST CENTURY, experts have inundated us with lectures and books about white privilege. According to one such expert, Layla F. Saad, "White supremacy is arguably the most complex social system of the last several hundred years."[1] White privilege, or rather, the evil of white privilege/white supremacy, is being taught in our schools and not just in universities. Are there white people who believe they are better than others because of the colour of their skin? Yes. And we are working hard to undo the damage of those beliefs. There is no doubt that in America tens of thousands of people came to believe that black people were "lesser than" in an earlier age.

White children, raised in the south by loving black nannies, nannies who often spent more time with them than their own mothers, grew up to be racist. They loved their nannies. Yet, they grew up to demand of other black nannies that they use different toilets, different water fountains, different shops and theatres, a regular apartheid style of life. How do you grow

---

1 Layla F. Saad, *Me and White Supremacy: Combat Racism, Change the World, and Become a Good Ancestor,* Thorndike Press, December 2020.

up loving your black nanny and then treating all black people as unequal?

This is another example of a cultural meme. Growing up in a family, a community, a society, including in the church that taught separation of the races, which dehumanized the black population, meant that it is only natural that one would automatically think this way unless something happened to alter one's perspective.

What is most astonishing to me is the speed with which one of these memes can enter the collective unconscious of a society. Slavery, the treatment of black people as something other than human, came to North America about 400 years ago. Although legally banned in 1865, some repercussions of this practice remain today.

Seems we have not learned the lesson from those past biases. Today, it is acceptable to attack white people for being born white and, therefore, innately superior and privileged.

Who are these "experts" whose books are being promoted to teachers and schools and the rest of society? Is the plan to teach this hate for white people, people of no color, for decades until the hate is innate—a cultural meme? The *New York Times* and *Esquire* contributor, Damon Young, wrote:

> Whiteness is a public health crisis. It shortens life expectancies, it pollutes air, it constricts equilibrium, it devastates forests, it melts ice caps, it sparks (and funds) wars, it flattens dialects, it infests consciousnesses, and it kills people, white people and people who are not white, my mom included. There will be people who die, in 2050, because of white supremacy-induced decisions from 1850.[2]

Another purveyor of this "racism" is Layla F. Saad in her book, *Me and White Supremacy*, a resource for white people (quoted above). The book came about following her free month-long Instagram challenge during the summer of 2018. She knew her audience. Her book has also been recommend-

---

2 Damon Young, "Whiteness Is a Pandemic," *The Root*, March 1, 2021.

ed for teachers to read so they can look inside themselves and find that active and passive racism that lurks within, and work diligently to remove it. She describes herself as an East African, Black, Muslim woman, born in Cardiff, Wales, living for a time in Great Britain, before moving with her family to Qatar, where she now lives with her husband and children. She thinks of herself as sitting at "a unique intersection of identities" from where she can help white people "work with the intention of creating a new world where Black, Indigenous, and People of Colour (BIPOC) live with dignity and equality" and remove "oppression and marginalization."

In photos, Saad is seen wearing a hijab which indicates she probably takes her Muslim faith seriously. What does that mean? First, it means she is not equal to her husband, brother, father or son. She may be oppressed at home by her own family. According to Amnesty International in Qatar 2021:

> Women continued to face discrimination in law and practice. Under the guardianship system, women remained tied to their male guardian, usually their father, brother, grandfather or uncle, or for married women, to their husband. Women continued to need their guardian's permission for key life decisions to marry, study abroad on government scholarships, work in many government jobs, travel abroad until certain ages, and receive some forms of reproductive healthcare.

> Family laws continued to discriminate against women by making it difficult for them to divorce. Divorced women remained unable to act as their children's guardian.[3]

She may not see it that way, may not be aware of her oppression/suppression, but male supremacy is the way of life in Islam. Twenty-five percent of the world is Muslim.

Saad comes from a belief system that sees all non-Muslims as second class. Lesser than. Non-Muslims do not have

---

3 Amnesty International Report: Qatar 2021. https://www.amnesty.org/en/location/middle-east-and-north-africa/qatar/report-qatar/.

equal rights with Muslims. It is called *dhimmitude*. As a Muslim woman, she has privilege over non-Muslims. In the past, during the caliphates, Jews had to wear yellow stars on their clothing to be easily identified. Sound familiar?

Saad says a prayer, the *Al Fatiha*, five times a day that demeans, denigrates and dehumanizes Jews and Christians. As for its virtue, it is narrated from Muhammad:

> The reward of any Muslim who recites the Surah 'Opening', is like that of a person who has recited two thirds of the Qur'an, and so much reward would he receive as if he has given every believing Muslim, man or woman, a free will offering.[4]

The *Al Fatiha* states:

> In the name of God, the infinitely Compassionate and Merciful.
> Praise be to God, Lord of all the worlds.
> The Compassionate, the Merciful. Ruler on the Day of Reckoning.
> You alone do we worship, and You alone do we ask for help.
> Guide us on the straight path,
> the path of those who have received your grace;
> not the path of those who have brought down wrath, nor of those who wander astray.
> Amen.[5]

It is generally accepted that "those who wander astray" refers to the Christians and "those who have brought down wrath" refers to the Jews.

This idea was formed because of the different responses of these two groups to Islam in its early years. The Qur'an clearly states that the Jews held an enmity toward Islam and were

---

4 Shaykh Tabarsi, *Majma'-ul-Bayan fi-Tafsir al-Qur'an*, vol. 1, p. 17.

5 Surah Al-Fatihah, Chapter 1. See: https://www.al-islam.org/enlightening-commentary-light-holy-quran-vol-1/surah-al-fatihah-chapter-1.

among the first to reject Muhammad's claim of prophethood. They were also among the first to be attacked by Muhammad's army; therefor, they are "those who have brought down wrath."

The Christians, however, were misled because of their supposed misperception of Islam and religion in general and, therefore, they were rendered as "those gone astray." Christians believe in the Trinity instead of pure monotheism—the worship of one God (Allah) alone.

All the commentators agree "those who earn the anger" are the Jews, and "those who go astray" are the Christians.

Yet, Saad is an expert on white supremacy.

She has lived for some time in Qatar. The country hosting the 2022 FIFA World Cup (soccer). Qatar routinely turns to countries like Nepal, India, Bangladesh and others in Southeast Asia and Africa to find cheap labour. It is estimated there are 1.4m migrant workers in Qatar (approximately 88% of the population).[6] They are exploited by the "kafala system," a system that the government has pledged to dismantle. Under Qatar's "kafala" (Arabic word for sponsorship) system, migrant workers must obtain their employer's permission in the form of a no-objection certificate (NOC) before changing jobs. This is a law that rights activists say ties employees to their employers and leads to abuse and exploitation. Recruiters seek out unemployed foreigners who need work to feed families. They promise relatively well-paying jobs in Qatar. The unemployed foreigners, envisioning ample wages they will soon be sending home, take out loans to pay off the recruiters. In return, they claim one of these coveted jobs abroad.[7]

But in doing so, these people essentially sign their life away to Qatari companies. The companies all but own them, which is why experts have likened the system to slavery. The migrants live in cramped, filthy labor camps. They can't leave for another

---

6 Wesley Stephenson, "Have 1,200 World Cup workers really died in Qatar?" *BBC Radio 4*, June 6, 2015.

7 See Amnesty International, "Migrants building a state-of-the-art stadium for the 2022 football World Cup in Qatar are abused and exploited – while FIFA makes huge profits," undated.

job or go home without permission from authorities.

They are reportedly paid around $200 or $300 a month, unless their owners don't feel like paying them, in which case they have little recourse. The average income for a citizen in Qatar in 2019 was US $64,781.00. In Bangladesh, it is $1,855.00. In India, it is $2,104.00 and in Pakistan, $1,284.00.[8]

Qatar, it is clear, could pay its workers decently. It boasts the highest GDP per capita in the world, and a 12-figure sovereign wealth fund.[9]

Qatar is in the midst of changing these "laws."

Yet, this woman is an expert on white supremacy.

Now, if this book doesn't help, you can try one of the 40 on this list that provides this advice:

> Lots of books will make you feel comfortable with your whiteness and whiteness in general, even for people of color. Authors have been sparing your feelings and treating you like porcelain, but it's time to let the bull loose in the proverbial china shop. White fragility needs to take a back seat. Fall back Karen. (For those unfamiliar with this use of Karen; Karen is a pejorative term for a white woman seeming to be entitled or demanding beyond the scope of what is normal. The term also refers to memes depicting white women who use their privilege to demand their own way). It's time to talk about dismantling white supremacy culture and bringing folks of color (the global majority) to the center.[10]

You, too, can participate in teaching your non-racialized child—born with white skin—that he needs to look into his heart and see the evil. It has nothing to do with his soul—only the colour of his skin.

---

8 Data from the World Bank. https://data.worldbank.org/indicator/NY.GDP.PCAP.CD?locations=QA.

9 Henry Bushnell, "Quasi-slavery is building Qatar's 2022 World Cup stadiums, and FIFA is fine with it," *Yahoo Sports*, June 11, 2020.

10 See: "40+ Books for AntiRacist Teachers – White Fragiles Beware! (2022 update)," https://culturallyresponsiveleadership.com/antiracistbooks/.

It is one thing to have individuals preach demonization of whiteness, denigrating people based on colour—or is it lack of colour? What is far more detrimental and frightening is that this hatred has been shared in a museum in America.

In 2020, the National Museum of African American History and Culture included a presentation entitled "Talking About Race." A chart included in the section titled "Aspects and Assumptions of Whiteness in the United States," included unwanted cultural attitudes such as "hard work is the key to success" and damaging cultural ideas such as "objective, rational linear thinking."

> White dominant culture, or whiteness, refers to the ways white people and their traditions, attitudes, and ways of life have been normalized over time and are now considered standard practices in the United States. And since white people still hold most of the institutional power in America, we have all internalized some aspects of white culture — including people of color.

> According to the chart, aspects of whiteness included self-reliance, a nuclear family where the husband is the 'breadwinner' and the wife is a 'homemaker,' no tolerance for deviation from single god concept, respecting authority, planning for the future and 'bland is best' in aesthetics.[11]

The National Museum of African American History and Culture is attacking the family? Demeaning breadwinning husbands? Attacking respect for authority? The Museum added: "Education is core to our mission." Really? That is their motto? What exactly do they think they are teaching? What would Martin Luther King Jr. say if he visited this museum funded by American taxpayers today? An organization meant to stop the spread of racism based on skin colour shares information about white people that they consider... what? Oppressive?

---

11 Chacour Koop, "Smithsonian museum apologizes for saying hard work, rational thought is 'white culture,'" *Miami Herald*, July 17, 2020.

Not to worry. The Museum apologized for the chart listing hard work and rational thought as traits of white culture after a media firestorm ensued.

We are left to wonder why individuals like Layla F. Saad and many more authors continue to share anti-white rhetoric in the name of Progress. Why not? There are no real repercussions for sharing this type of hate. On the contrary, for many it is the very ticket to both academic and popular acclaim.

14

Who are these white privileged people, the victimizers?

T HE NEW WORLD has been populated by millions of people from all over the Old World. Millions were white. Many were poor, starving, uneducated, attacked and often ridiculed at home. These are the ancestors of the white privileged oppressors. These included Ukrainians who migrated to Canada, most of whom became farmers. In America the Ukrainians worked in the mines,[1] but all came from the same place—extreme poverty and hunger.

The population of immigrants born in European countries other than those of the British Isles started to increase in the late 1800s, slowly at first and then more rapidly, peaking in the 1970s. The first wave began in the late 1800s and early 1900s, with the arrival of new groups of immigrants from Eastern Europe (Russians, Polish and Ukrainians), Western Europe and Scandinavia.

A second immigration boom following World War II continued to favour immigration from the British Isles, but a significant number of immigrants also arrived from Western Europe (Germany and the Netherlands) and Southern Europe (Italy, Greece, Yugoslavia and Portugal) from

---

1   See: Marianne P. Fedunkiw, "Ukrainian americans," *Countries and their Cultures*, 2006.

the 1950s to the 1970s. At the time of the 1971 Census, 28.3% of immigrants were born in the United Kingdom and 51.4% were born in another European country.[2]

Ukrainian immigrants make up one of the largest groups to come to Canada.[3] Poor and starving at home, the peasantry had been harassed and abused by Russian soldiers posted throughout the Ukraine and kept in a state of third-world poverty compounded by a drought and a famine.

They were mostly farmers, and Canada needed hardy farming settlers to build the West. At first, a few thousand men, woman and children, most of whom had nothing but the clothes on their backs, no education and very little money, were sent by train to the plains of Saskatchewan and Alberta where they were given two draft horses and a cart each, along with some basic farming tools and food supplies, and shown their plot of land. Sounded great but was often nothing more than a barren desert or a large plot of forest that had to be cleared. But the land was ploughed and planted.

More Ukrainians arrived during the Great Depression, a dismal time to arrive looking for a better life, but eventually found work in industry, forestry and mining, with most of them settling in Ontario.

The Ukrainian-Canadians make up 10 percent of the country's population.

Another class of "oppressors," the Irish, often called Micks, arrived during the first half of the nineteenth century. By the 1850s, more than 500,000 Irish had immigrated to British North America.

Many Irish immigrants landed in Newfoundland, where they worked as fishermen and lived in the kind of dire poverty they had hoped to escape when they left the Old World. In the middle of the nineteenth century, the Irish provided cheap

---

2 "150 years of immigration in Canada," *Statistics Canada*. https://www150. statcan.gc.ca/n1/pub/11-630-x/11-630-x2016006-eng.htm.

3 "The Ukrainians," *Canada Alive*, July 12, 2013. https://canadaalive.wordpress.com/2013/07/12/the-ukrainians/.

labour in the cities, as well as working on the many public construction projects underway at that time.

The Irish Potato Famine of the late 1840s drove 1.5 to 2 million destitute Irish out of Ireland.[4]

These immigrants arrived in large numbers and in poor physical condition, coming over in what has been described as "coffin ships." They took this trip in order to be free of British oppression.

More than 38,000 migrants escaping the famine landed on Toronto's waterfront. The sheer number of poor and often ill immigrants strained local resources. Initially, the refugees landed on a wharf near the present-day site of the Metro Toronto Convention Centre. Eleven hundred died from typhus or other illnesses.[5]

Those who survived supplied cheap labour that helped fuel the economic expansion of the 1850s and 1860s. They were poor and resented because of the urban and rural squalor in which they were forced to live. The hostility toward the Irish was widespread.

In 1858, a *Globe* columnist described the Irish as "lazy, improvident and unthankful; they fill our poor houses and our prisons."[6]

In the twentieth century, there were still signs that read "no Irish need apply."

More "white oppressor" Jewish refugees tried to come to Canada and the US prior to the Shoah. The Jewish people are not white; rather they come in many colours and races and 90% can trace their DNA to the Levant. Those who made it to these shores, many penniless, were grateful to be out of Europe and Russia. Russian Jews emigrated seeking relief from ghet-

4 See: Jamie Bradburn, "Irish Potato Famine Refugees," *The Canadian Encyclopedia.* https://www.thecanadianencyclopedia.ca/en/article/toronto-feature-irish-potato-famine-refugees.

5 See: Harold Troper, "Immigration to Canada," *The Canadian Encyclopedia. https://www.thecanadianencyclopedia.ca/en/article/immigration.*

6 Mark G. McGowan, *The Waning of the Green: Catholics, the Irish, and Identity in Toronto, 1887-1922 (Volume 32)*, McGill-Queen's University Press, 1998, p. 17.

to life and the pogroms of western Russia. My father arrived when he was thirteen. He had witnessed the death of a young boy during one of the many pogroms in his village. My mother was first-generation Canadian. She was told by her high school teacher to change her name so she could get work. Her name was too Jewish.

Canada was rife with anti-Semitism in the '30s and '40s. Tensions exploded in the Christie Pits Riot of 1933.[7] In a 1946 Gallup poll, well after the horrors of Auschwitz were widely known, Canadians were asked to make a list of undesirable immigrants. Jews finished in second place, behind the Japanese who had attacked Pearl Harbour, as the least desirable immigrants.[8] In cottage country, and even on Toronto's beaches until the mid-1950s, it was common to see signs that read "No Dogs or Jews Allowed."

My favourite sign: Gentiles Only.

Most of the early immigrants from Russia were peasants who found work in various industries. After WWI, many of the one million Russians (the majority of them agricultural and industrial labourers) fleeing the effects of the Russian Revolution sought admission to Canada to work as farm labourers, loggers and miners.

The six discernable waves of Polish immigration to Canada were from 1854-1901, 1902-15, 1916-39, 1944-56, 1957-79 and 1980-93.[9] Hard-working, religious peasants, many received land grants from the government or bought lots in Manitoba, Saskatchewan and Alberta, where they built farms. Others worked on railway construction or in the coal mines. The second generation very often moved to larger settlements or towns, where they opened small businesses.

The Irish were called Micks. The Jews were called Kikes.

---

7 Daniel Bitonti, "Remembering Toronto's Christie Pits Riot," *The Globe and Mail*, August 9, 2013.

8 Gerald Tulchinsky, *Canada's Jews: A People's Journey*, University of Toronto Press, 2008, p. 403.

9 Benedykt Heydenkorn, "Polish Canadians," *The Canadian Encyclopedia*. https://www.thecanadianencyclopedia.ca/en/article/poles.

And then there is my father's story—not much different from many other fathers and mothers who came to America and Canada.

He was born in September 1907. He had two brothers and a sister. He had come to Canada when he was young to be with an older brother who was already here. I don't know when the other siblings arrived. The family came from a place called Sasov—sometimes in Poland and sometimes in Russia. I think it was mostly Poland when he lived there, because he spoke Polish Yiddish while my mother spoke Russian Yiddish, and they used to argue over the word for spoon. I know my mother's history is Russian, so that's how I concluded that Sasov was more influenced by Poland than Russia.

I can't find Sasov on a map. Google has no idea what I am asking. In the 1880's and 1890's, after the assassination of Russian Tsar Alexander II, Russian-Polish Jews were exposed to a series of organized massacres targeting Jewish communities called pogroms. After WWI, Poland became an even more hostile place for many Jews. A series of pogroms and discriminatory laws were signs of growing antisemitism, while fewer and fewer opportunities to emigrate were available. My father lived through the pogroms. He witnessed children being shot. Perhaps that's the reason he was sent to Canada.

I didn't learn about my father until after he and my mother died. The stories he didn't tell me were in the records I found. The pieces of paper he kept. Perhaps we need to have a list of prepared questions for each newborn to ask their parents while still alive.

The most important piece of paper is on my bookshelf: his ticket to Canada from Glasgow, Scotland, August 21, 1920, aboard the ship the *S.S. Sicilian*.

It had previously been chartered as a troop ship for the Boer War. According to the ship documents, he landed in Quebec or Montreal. The ship was owned by Canadian Pacific at that time. He would have been one of 900 third-class passengers. A privilege. My father would have been turning 13 that September. It just occurred to me as I am writing about him that I don't know if he had a bar mitzvah. And if he did – where and with whom?

From Glasgow, my father made it to Toronto to be with his older brother. How did my father get from Sasov, Poland, to Scotland and on to Toronto? He was 12 years old and I know he came alone. As far as I am aware, he didn't speak English.

My dad probably felt privileged to leave Sasov—terrified, but privileged. How he got from his shtetl to a town where he could board a train—I assume it was a train, to take him to I don't know where; I have no idea. What documents did he have? Did he have a suitcase? What did he bring with him from home to take to the New World? What did he eat? Where did he sleep? How long did it take? And then to arrive alive in Scotland. How did he cross the English Channel? And from what port? He probably felt privileged to go steerage class on the Sicilian. He would have been one of 900 steerage passengers, cramped together in dark and damp quarters below decks along with the rats and insects and disease. His meals would have been meat, generally old, tough, and bad smelling. The fish not much better. The trip across the Atlantic took between one and two weeks. I know he thanked God when he made it to Canada. That was a privilege.

Then came earning a living. At thirteen. These are stories I was never told, but I know there was no free ride. He didn't go to school.

He wanted to be a musician. He lived in Detroit for a while. He played the saxophone. I have a photo of him on my bookshelf with his saxophone. But he wasn't good enough to make a living from it.

He opened a business and met my mother, and the two of them worked hard to raise their children and send them to university so that they could live a better life. He probably considered this a privilege. To do what he wanted without being shot. To work hard and live long enough to see his grandchildren and know that they would be safe.

When I was eight or nine years old, my dad and I were in the basement where I had a blackboard. He asked me to teach him to read. Imagine that. He could read but not the way he wanted to read. He wanted to be better. I remember him crying when he asked. My mother told me that my Dad began to read a great deal when he retired. I am blessed to have his books. I know he suffered from depression with bouts of mania. I learned after he died that he tried to kill himself at 16. What drove a 16-year-old to try and take his life after all he had experienced and suffered to come to Canada? Is this what happens when you live a privileged life?

When my father came to Canada to continue with his privileged life, he changed his name from Avraham, on the ship's manifest, to Allan. He met my mother in Toronto. Her birth name was Sarah, but in order to continue with her privileged life, she changed it to Susan so people would not know she was Jewish. Her high school teacher told her to do that. My mother was lucky. Her father wanted her to quit school when she could spell cat and rat—that was the joke at home. But my grandmother, a tiny woman, insisted that she finish high school. She was privileged.

I tell you this because I am the proud daughter of Avraham and Sarah (named after the first two Jews). It is a privilege.

My grandchildren tell me about being privileged. That's what they are told in school. As if everything had been handed to them on a silver platter. How dare they be so privileged? I wonder what my father would say to his great-grandchildren about the meaning of privilege. I think he would have told them that we are not the object of our lives. Life does not happen to us. We are the subject; we have the right and the obligation to make choices to better ourselves and others. And it is in that choosing that we bring dignity to our lives.

I wonder what my father would say if he saw people bending the knee to others in shame for being so privileged after everything he survived, never complaining, perhaps pretending it never happened?

These are just some of the white "privileged" people who came to Canada and America. Their privilege: getting out of their Old World countries with the promise of freedom in the

New World. Coming to this new place with gratitude and hope for a better future based on their character, not their characteristics. What they did not pack in their bags were victimhood or entitlement.

Today, we are taught that white people, meaning colonizers and oppressors, brought evil to the indigenous peoples, as if the indigenous peoples were peace-loving, caring and non-violent.

Let's take a look at history rather than share wishful thinking:

> In the 1640s, the Iroquois launched regular attempts to destroy Huron fur expeditions, followed by direct attacks on the weakened Huron settlements. The campaign of 1648-1649 literally destroyed the Huron nation. A few Huron survivors managed to reach Montreal with the Jesuits, but most were adopted into the Iroquois nations, as was customary. The Huron-Iroquois wars and the destruction of Huronia are very precisely recorded in the Jesuits' annual reports.[10]

Intertribal rivalries aside:

> What you probably don't picture are Cherokee slaveholders, foremost among them Cherokee chief John Ross. What you probably don't picture are the numerous African-American slaves, Cherokee-owned, who made the brutal march themselves, or else were shipped en masse to what is now Oklahoma aboard cramped boats by their wealthy Indian masters.
>
> (...)
>
> In the case of the Trail of Tears and the enslavement of blacks by prominent members of all five so-called "Civilized Tribes" (Cherokee, Chickasaw, Choctaw, Creek and Seminole), [National Museum of the American Indian curator Paul Chaat] Smith went one step further, likening the ugly truth of history to a "mangy, snarling dog stand-

---

10 "Huron-Iroquois War," http://option.canada.pagesperso-orange.fr/ huron-iroquois.htm.

ing between you and a crowd-pleasing narrative."
(...)
[Smith continued,] "The Five Civilized Tribes were deeply committed to slavery, established their own racialized black codes, immediately re-established slavery when they arrived in Indian territory, rebuilt their nations with slave labor, crushed slave rebellions, and enthusiastically sided with the Confederacy in the Civil War."[11]

Tell me again about white supremacy/privilege. We have come full circle.

> I have a dream that my four children will one day live in a nation where they will not be judged by the colour of their skin, but by the content of their character.
> —Martin Luther King Jr., August 28, 1963.

The late Rabbi Jonathan Sacks wrote about covenant in his book, *Morality*. He wrote: "Covenant is about what we have in common despite our differences. It speaks to us as activist citizens sharing collective responsibility. It is not the politics of 'Us' against 'Them;' it is the politics of 'all of us together.'"[12]

Our society is devolving. Western culture is declining.
We have become a house divided. And a house divided will fall.

---

11 Ryan P. Smith, "How Native American Slaveholders Complicate the Trail of Tears Narrative," *The Smithsonian*, March 6, 2018.

12 Jonathan Sacks, *Morality: Restoring the Common Good in Divided Times,* Basic Books, 2020, Chapter 23.

15

Dear Parents:
Speak up before it is too late

Some people try to be tall by cutting off the heads of others.
—Paramahansa Yogananda

I BUMPED INTO the classmate who had tattled on me more than 50 years earlier. She wanted to apologize for what she had done. No need. She had done me a favor. I had learned an important lesson. I would never let anyone bully me again. I would never let anyone force me to say something that was not true. I would never be bullied into silence or submission.

I grew into a woman who refuses to be silenced, to submit, to bend the knee to some false god in the name of diversity, inclusion, accommodation, equity or any other moral or ethical system that does not include the Judeo-Christian ethic—the only ethic that demands freedom, moral agency and the sanctity of all life. I knew at that moment that I would never let anyone bully me into silence again and that someday when I was a mother, no one in power would be bullying my children.

Bullying in school has morphed over time. Now the teachers are the bullies—pushing "woke" policies not that much different from promoting racism, separating people based on characteristics, not character. Traditionally, teachers have tried

145

to empower kids, but now the curricula aims to foster tribalism, anger, resentment, and victimhood. As Children's Educational Opportunity Foundation President Lewis Andrews writes, "Sadly, today's woke curricula do far more to erode a child's sense of intrinsic worth than to build it up. One can hardly imagine a more effective way of grooming disorganized and incompetent adults."[1]

In Buffalo, New York, public schools, a curriculum has been designed requiring schools to teach the "Black Lives Matter principles," including "dismantling cisgender privilege," creating "queer-affirming network[s] where heteronormative thinking no longer exists," and accelerating "the disruption of Western nuclear family dynamics. As one veteran teacher in the Buffalo Public School system recently put it, anti-racist classrooms have devolved into little more than a series of 'scoldings, guilt-trips, and demands to demean oneself simply to make another feel empowered.'"[2]

New York's East Side Community School is encouraging white parents to become "white traitors" and advocate for "white abolition:"

> There are eight stages of white identity development—from the lowest form, "white supremacist," to the intermediate forms of "white confessional" and "white traitor," to the highest form, "white abolitionist." The goal of this process, according to the graphic's creator, Northwestern University professor Barnor Hesse, is challenging the "regime of whiteness" and eventually to "subvert white authority" and "not [allow] whiteness to reassert itself."[3]

Imagine being a white child, today. The shame of it all. And nothing can be done to alleviate the shame.

---

1 Lewis M. Andrews, "The Other Problem with Woke Schooling: It's Psychological Child Abuse," *Real Clear Policy*, April 06, 2021.

2 Christopher F. Rufo, "Failure Factory," *City Journal*, February 23, 2021.

3 Christopher F. Rufo, "Gone Crazy," *City Journal*, February 18, 2021.

In Los Angeles, the school district is considering a curriculum that disdains "merit" and "individualism," and claims that "history classes and textbooks focus on the perspective of white colonial culture."

In the San Diego Unified School District, students must "confront and examine your white privilege" and to "acknowledge when you feel white fragility." Additionally, children are told to "understand the impact of white supremacy in your work."[4]

Princeton University has entered the discussion. The Diversity, Equity and Inclusion (I prefer to refer to it as DIE: diversity, inclusion, equity) office of Princeton University greeted the freshman class of 2021 with a video/site which:

[I]ncludes a two-minute discourse in which classics professor Dan-el Padilla Peralta characterizes free speech as a "privilege," rather than a right, and in which he disparages the speech of others with whom he disagrees as "masculine-ized bravado." Padilla Peralta goes on to extol "free speech and intellectual discourse that is [sic] flexed to one specific aim, and that aim is the promotion of social justice, and an anti-racist social justice at that."[5]

The attacks on Western Culture have become so commonplace that comments like these are made without shame or fear. And, too often, not refuted.

A number of black intellectuals now openly envision American life segregated from whites. *The Nation's* Elie Mystal envisions his life as "whiteness-free."[6]

Imagine how non-colored children will feel when they

4 Larry Sand, "Child Abuse in Plain Sight," *American Greatness*, April 14, 2021.

5 John Londregan and Sergiu Klainerman, "Profs: Princeton diversity office's 'nihilistic' attack on university's history and anti-woke dissidents," *New York Post*, September 1, 2021.

6 Elie Mystal, "I Am Not Ready to Reenter White Society," *The Nation*, March 23, 2021.

hear this? How afraid will they become? And how will that fear affect their mental well-being?

Our children in university are being taught to stifle free speech. Chicago University student author Kelly Hui wrote:

> [E]mphasis on free speech, which is so often used as a right-wing talking point opens up room for bigoted language and bigoted actions, and how university administrations—including our own—enable this. In a post-insurrection society, we must re-examine the Chicago principles and find a way to balance freedom of academic inquiry with protecting our marginalized students and creating an inclusive community for all.[7]

Pardon me? Free speech has become a right-wing talking point? Students of color need protecting in a university? How demeaning. By the time one gets to university, a student should be educated enough to stand up for their beliefs and debate them.

For those unaware of the Chicago principles, here is a glimpse.

> From its very founding, the University of Chicago has dedicated itself to the preservation and celebration of the freedom of expression as an essential element of the University's culture... President Hanna Holborn Gray observed that 'education should not be intended to make people comfortable, it is meant to make them think. Universities should be expected to provide the conditions within which hard thought, and therefore strong disagreement, independent judgment, and the questioning of stubborn assumptions, can flourish in an environment of the greatest freedom'... Because the University is committed to free and open inquiry in all matters, it guarantees all members of the University community the broadest possible latitude to speak, write, listen, challenge, and learn. Except insofar as limitations on that freedom are necessary to the functioning of the

---

7   Kelly Hui, "Instructing Insurrections: How UChicago Can Avoid Creating the Next Ted Cruz," *The Chicago Maroon*, January 24, 2021.

University, the University of Chicago fully respects and supports the freedom of all members of the University community 'to discuss any problem that presents itself.'[8]

Rikki Schlott is a writer and student based in New York City. She works for *The Megyn Kelly Show* and has been published by *The Daily Wire* and *The Conservative Review*. She wrote: "Generation Z is suffering a less obvious and more insidious crisis of free expression. This is reflected in a recent survey by Heterodox Academy that found 62 percent of college students feel the climate on their campus prevents them from saying what they believe, up from 55 percent in 2019."[9] Is it any wonder?

Now is the time, dear parents and grandparents, to wake up to the "woke" agenda that has infiltrated public and private schools from kindergarten to grade 12 and on to university, across America and now the world. Your children, of every race and color, are being exposed to child abuse.

For far too long, black people were looked upon as "lesser than." They were judged by color, not competence. Today, despite the fact that we know the immorality and the illegality of racism, we are being dragged back into a race war. And people of color are going to suffer the most because they are being taught that they cannot keep up with people of no color and will require special treatment.

Progressives no longer talk about the root causes of disparity; they have distilled it into two groups: Black and white with no shades of grey. This "woke" ideology promoted by BLM and CRT is abusive, emotionally and psychologically. It is your job, your primary job, your most important job, to protect your children from hate. Too many are remaining silent. Jack Fowler of the *National Review* wrote: "We have seen at other institu-

---

8 University of Chicago, *Report of the Committee on Freedom of Expression*, https://provost.uchicago.edu/sites/default/files/documents/reports/FOE-CommitteeReport.pdf.

9 Rikki Schlott, "Generation Z's Silent Free Speech Crisis," *The Epoch Times*, April 4, 2021.

tions that when a school restructures its educational philosophy around the principles of CRT, free and open debate is quickly replaced by a climate of fear and silence."[10]

This attack on non-colored people is no different than the attacks on people of color over the centuries. Yet, the same people who call themselves victims are victimizing non-colored people. Could it not lead to cultural PTSD in white families as has been suggested in black families?[11] You must defend your children from this:

> [C]ult-like dogma that deliberately shames, denigrates and segregates children, compels speech, disallows dissent and uses rhetorical manipulation to bully teachers and students into compliance...
> (...)
> We passed a law in 1964 to outlaw racial discrimination in public spaces. That law still applies today. The law passed in 1972 to eliminate sex discrimination in education applies today. The first amendment protects Americans from compelled speech in addition to granting the freedom to speak.[12]

As Thomas Sowell has written:

> Ours may become the first civilization destroyed, not by the power of our enemies, but by the ignorance of our teachers and the dangerous nonsense they are teaching our children. In an age of artificial intelligence, they are creating artificial stupidity.[13]

---

10 Jack Fowler, "Another Prestigious School Pummeled by Critical Race Theory," *National Review*, April 28, 2021.

11 See, for example, Jacquelyn Clemmons, "Black Families Have Inherited Trauma, but We Can Change That," *Healthline*, August 26, 2020.

12 Erika Sanzi, "The Coming Bipartisan Backlash to Public School Wokeness," *Newsweek*, April 20, 2021.

13 Quotations of the day from Thomas Sowell, *American Enterprise Institute*. https://www.aei.org/carpe-diem/quotations-of-the-day-from-thomas-sowell-4/.

Pink Floyd's lyrics from "Another Brick in the Wall" (*The Wall*), 1979, remain timely, today.

> We don't need no education
> We don't need no thought control
> No dark sarcasm in the classroom
> Teacher, leave them kids alone
> Hey, teacher, leave them kids alone

Take heart in the actions already taken by parents who have seen the damage done to their children. Do not fear. You are the parent!

> In a suit filed in the U.S. District Court for the District of Nevada on December 20, 2020, Gabrielle Clark, the mother of William Clark, a twelfth-grader in a Nevada charter school, complained about the school's refusal to accept her son's objection to what was being taught in a recently revised civics course. Ms. Clark, a widow, is black. Her son's father, however, was white, and her son was light-skinned enough to be considered white.
>
> In her complaint, Clark stated that a new curriculum at William's school inserted consciousness raising and conditioning exercises under the banner of 'Intersectionality' and 'Critical Race Theory.' The lesson categorized certain racial and religious identities as inherently 'oppressive,' . . . and instructed pupils including William Clark who fell into these categories to accept the label 'oppressor.'
>
> Despite Clark's and her son's objections to what he was being required to admit about himself and his racial heritage, the school insisted that he take this course and gave him a failing grade — imperiling his chances for college admission — because of his refusal to admit that he harbored the views that were being pressed upon the class.[14]

---

14 Peter J. Wallison, "Critical Race Theory: The Enemy of Reason, Evidence, and Open Debate," *National Review*, April 26, 2021.

Isn't this emotional abuse?

Parents of students at Regis, a Jesuit school, rebelled against plans to incorporate a curriculum to "educate all your students about the realities of race, power, and privilege in America." A letter was sent.

> This is an open letter from a group of concerned alumni and parents. Up until July 8th of last year, we were thankful that Regis remained faithful to its mission of academic excellence and fostering a spirit of generosity and service to those in need, and had resisted the fashionable racism inherent in Critical Race Theory (CRT) that has been embraced by other educational institutions. We felt confident that the academic rigor and focus on critical thinking that Regis has instilled in its graduates for over a century made Regis immune to the anti-rational, anti-liberal, anti-meritocratic, neo-racist ideology that is Critical Race Theory... Unless alumni speak up, we fear our Interim President, the to-be-hired Director of DEI, and the Diversity Steering Committee are going to do irreparable damage to our alma mater, despite their good intentions. CRT advocates work to weaken or eliminate entrance exams, reduce curricular focus on the Western Canon, set firm racial quotas for students and faculty (regardless of qualifications), and achieve "Equity" (equality of outcomes) by reducing all students' performance to that of the weakest.[15]

Andrew Guttman, a parent at Brearley, a private all-girls school on the Upper East Side of Manhattan which costs $54,000 a year, took umbrage with a demand that prospective parents had to take an anti-racist pledge before being considered for admission. He removed his child from the school. Here is part of the letter he wrote to other parents:

> We no longer have confidence that our daughter will receive the quality of education necessary to further her

---

15   Jack Fowler, "Another Prestigious School Pummeled by Critical Race Theory," *National Review*, April 28, 2021.

development into a critically thinking, responsible, enlightened, and civic minded adult...

It cannot be stated strongly enough that Brearley's obsession with race must stop. It should be abundantly clear to any thinking parent that Brearley has completely lost its way. The administration and the Board of Trustees have displayed a cowardly and appalling lack of leadership by appeasing an anti-intellectual, illiberal mob, and then allowing the school to be captured by that same mob. What follows are my own personal views on Brearley's antiracism initiatives, but these are just a handful of the criticisms that I know other parents have expressed.

I object to the view that I should be judged by the color of my skin. I cannot tolerate a school that not only judges my daughter by the color of her skin, but encourages and instructs her to prejudge others by theirs. By viewing every element of education, every aspect of history, and every facet of society through the lens of skin color and race, we are desecrating the legacy of Dr. Martin Luther King Jr., and utterly violating the movement for which such civil rights leaders believed, fought, and died.

I object to the idea that Blacks are unable to succeed in this country without aid from government or from whites. Brearley, by adopting critical race theory, is advocating the abhorrent viewpoint that Blacks should forever be regarded as helpless victims, and are incapable of success regardless of their skills, talents, or hard work. What Brearley is teaching our children is precisely the true and correct definition of racism.

If Brearley's administration was truly concerned about so-called "equity," it would be discussing the cessation of admissions preferences for legacies, siblings, and those families with especially deep pockets. If the administration was genuinely serious about "diversity," it would not insist on the indoctrination of its students, and their families, to a single mindset, most reminiscent of the Chinese Cultural Revolution.

I object to Brearley's advocacy for groups and movements such as Black Lives Matter, a Marxist, anti family, heterophobic, anti-Asian and anti-Semitic organization that neither speaks for the majority of the Black community in this country, nor in any way, shape or form, represents their best interests.

The number one priority of a school has always been, and always will be, education. Brearley's misguided priorities exemplify both the safety culture and "cover-your-ass" culture that together have proved so toxic to our society and have so damaged the mental health and resiliency of two generations of children, and counting...

Lastly, I object, with as strong a sentiment as possible, that Brearley has begun to teach what to think, instead of how to think. I object that the school is now fostering an environment where our daughters, and our daughters' teachers, are afraid to speak their minds in class for fear of "consequences." I object that Brearley is trying to usurp the role of parents in teaching morality, and bullying parents to adopt that false morality at home. I object that Brearley is fostering a divisive community where families of different races, which until recently were part of the same community, are now segregated into two.

It is abundantly clear that the majority of parents believe that Brearley's antiracism policies are misguided, divisive, counterproductive and cancerous. Many believe, as I do, that these policies will ultimately destroy what was until recently, a wonderful educational institution. But as I am sure will come as no surprise to you, given the insidious cancel culture that has of late permeated our society, most parents are too fearful to speak up.

But speak up you must. There is strength in numbers and I assure you, the numbers are there.... For the sake of our community, our city, our country and most of all, our children, silence is no longer an option.[16]

16 Bari Weiss, "You Have to Read This Letter," *Common Sense*, April 16,

Harvey Goldman spoke up about his nine-year-old daughter's education at the $43,000-per-year Heschel School in Manhattan where she was learning about Black Lives Matter as well as her own "white privilege."

> First and foremost, neither I, nor my child, have 'white privilege,' nor do we need to apologize for it," Goldman wrote last September. "Suggesting I do is insulting. Suggesting to my 9-year-old child she does is child abuse, not education." In response, the school suggested Goldman take his daughter out of the school, he said. So he did.[17]

Another parent whose children were enrolled in the $54,000-a-year Riverdale Country School:

> Bion Bartning formed the Foundation Against Intolerance & Racism (FAIR) to combat CRT in schools and promote a "pro-human" agenda. More than 20,000 people have already joined.

> Bartning, who is Mexican and Yaqui on one side and Jewish on the other, said he was especially dismayed by how Riverdale and schools across the country force kids to label themselves based on their skin color. Sometimes kids are even given a palette and made to choose the color that best fits their skin, he said.[18]

Is this not abuse?

> Maud Maron, a public defender with four children in local public schools who is also running for City Council, said she first ran across the so-called anti-racist ideology more than five years ago as part of her work on the Community Education Council.
> (...)

2021.

17 Dana Kennedy, "Inside the growing underground network of parents fighting 'anti-racism' in NYC schools," *New York Post*, April 24, 2021.

18 Ibid.

Maron, who said her kids have been exposed to CRT in their public schools, said the ideology "may have started with some good intentions but now it's like a cult. If you don't go along with them, they think you are evil. But people should know that you can survive even if you speak out. Stand your ground and say what you believe. Don't apologize for simple truths.

(...)

Podcaster Megyn Kelly pulled her sons out of posh Collegiate last November after a letter allegedly circulated accusing white people of "reveling in state-sanctioned depravity" and comparing white children to "killer cops."[19]

Child abuse?

Harvey Goldman may be right when he suggested that teaching his daughter that she has white privilege is child abuse. She can't change her skin color. She had no control over her parentage or the actions of her parents, grandparents or great-grandparents. This is as abusive as telling children of color that they are victims of that color. Indeed:

> When youth are bullied because of something specific to their identity—like their religion, sexual orientation, or race, it very well may take a deeper emotional and psychological toll than bullying based on non-identity-related factors.[20]

This constant emotional maltreatment can have long-term impact on mental health, including devastating consequences for both the individual victim and for society as a whole.

> Emotional maltreatment can be broadly defined as "a repeated pattern of caregiver behavior or extreme incident(s) that convey to children that they are flawed, unloved, unwanted, endangered, or of value only in meeting another's needs." Researchers have speculated that

---

19 Ibid.

20 Sameer Hinduja, "Bullying Because of Religion: Our Latest Findings and Best Practices," *Cyberbullying Research Center*, undated.

emotional maltreatment is a core component underlying all forms of child maltreatment that has equivalent, if not greater, developmental consequences than childhood experiences of physical and/or sexual abuse.[21]

Think about that. The attacks on children based on skin color destroy the soul. We know that from past history. We are watching as young black people are being taught they are not as capable as white people; that in order to rise up they must tear down the other—bully. And we are witnessing impressionable young white children attacked for being white.

And these attacks are coming from so-called experts, professionals. Remember Dr. Moss? I introduced him in the Chapter on Revenge Racism. In his paper, "On Having Whiteness," Dr. Moss expressed the opinion that his race (white) has a "particular susceptibility" to being "parasites" and that white people have a sense of entitlement that has enabled them to seize power "without limit, force without restriction, violence without mercy," and can become terrorists as a result. Dr. Moss says interventions are required:

Such interventions can reasonably aim only to reshape Whiteness's infiltrated appetites — to reduce their intensity, redistribute their aims, and occasionally turn those aims toward the work of reparation. When remembered and represented, the ravages wreaked by the chronic condition can function either as warning ("never again") or as temptation ("great again"). Memorialization alone, therefore, is no guarantee against regression. There is not yet a permanent cure.[22]

Dorothy Evans Holmes, who is black, is professor emeritus of clinical psychology at The George Washington University

---

21 Tamara L.Taillieu, Douglas A. Brownridge, Jitender Sareen, Tracie O. Afifi, "Childhood emotional maltreatment and mental disorders: Results from a nationally representative adult sample from the United States," *Child Abuse & Neglect*, Volume 59, September 2016, Pages 1-12.

22 Quoted in Nick Monroe, "White people are parasites according to San Francisco psychologist," *Post Millennial*, June 9, 2021.

where she was program director and director of clinical training from 2005 to 2011. She is also a teaching, training and supervising analyst emeritus at the Baltimore Washington Institute for Psychoanalysis. July 1 of 2016, she was appointed teaching, training and supervising psychoanalyst at the Psychoanalytic Education Center of the Carolinas. She seems to agree with Dr. Moss's "concerns."

> I can only say that, for me, intellectual curiosity about and a need to deeply understand Whiteness were enough for me to agree to discuss this paper, knowing that uneasy feelings would likely be stirred in me by plunging into such untrodden territory.

> In exploring Whiteness, the search is for more than we already know and for more than we care to know. If we were to rely on theorized observation to study Whiteness, we would face the opportunities and biases of whichever theories we relied on. I would add that traditional psychoanalytic frames are particularly suspect because our history in psychoanalysis has been that we have appropriated those frames to perpetuate Whiteism. Here I use the word Whiteism to recognize Whiteness as action, in addition to its being a way or state of being. By use of Whiteism, we psychoanalysts have persistently and gratuitously privileged one theory over another and/or weaponized "theories" to hate - fully exclude or degrade disfavored sexualities and races.[23]

And then there is Dr. Aruna Khilanani, a psychiatrist who gave a lecture at Yale University's School of Medicine titled "The Psychopathic Problem of the White Mind" where she admitted that she sometimes fantasized about shooting white people, which has prompted a backlash against her and the university.[24] She defended her behavior as a means of expressing herself as a

---

23 Quoted in Andrea Widburg, "A peer-reviewed psychoanalytic journal publishes a grotesque anti-White screed," *American Thinker*, June 10, 2021.

24 Libby Emmons, "Yale's 'kill whitey' speech is not shocking—it's the new normal," *Post Millennial*, Jun 6, 2021.

person of Indian background![25]

This hate, because that is what it is, is being promoted by professionals in mental health. Your non-colored children are being told there is something very wrong with them. And they cannot fix it. Professionals are prepared to throw non-colored children under a bus. Who will protect them, if not their families?

Too many parents and grandparents are sitting back and defaulting on their role as protector of their families. They remain silent. Is it out of fear of being unliked on social media? Attacked as "racists" or as "white supremacists?" Your fear of being bullied, shunned and/or canceled, should not be greater than your efforts to protect your children of any color from bullying and child abuse at school at the hands of teachers and administrators. Do not sit back and allow the Mr. Salmons of the world to silence you.

---

25 Hannah Nightingale, "NYC psychiatrist who spoke on her 'fantasies' of killing white people defends controversial lecture," June 8, 2021.

16

Cancel Culture Cancels Family

Whatever the society, the culture or the faith, we need to teach our children, and they theirs, what we aspire to and the ideals we were bequeathed by those who came before us. We need to teach our children the story of which we and they are a part, and we need to trust them to go further than we did, when they come to write their own chapter.

—Rabbi Jonathan Sacks, remarks in the House of Lords on Friday 7th December 2017.

I F ONE VISITS the Black Lives Matter website, the first frame that comes up is a large crowd with fists raised and the slogan, "Now We Transform." Read the list of demands, and you get a sense of how deep a transformation they seek.

Black Lives Matter had posted on their website, which has since been removed: "We disrupt the Western-prescribed nuclear family structure requirement by supporting each other as extended families and 'villages' that collectively care for one another, especially our children, to the degree that mothers, parents, and children are comfortable."[1] According to Bill Pan at

---

1 Patrice Onwuka, "A BLM Vanishing Act: Its Webpage About Disrupting The Black Nuclear Family Is Gone," *Independent Women's Forum*, September 22, 2020.

The Epoch Times:

> [P]ublic school districts from Boston to Seattle are teaching lessons that correspond to core BLM values, such as "Diversity and Globalism," and "Trans-Affirming," "Queer Affirming," and "Collective Value."
> (...)
> According to the website for BLM at School,[2] the movement started in Seattle in 2016, when thousands of educators, along with hundreds of families and students, came to school wearing BLM shirts. The BLM at School curriculum has since been endorsed by a number of organizations and individuals, including the American Civil Liberties Union, National Education Association, and Boston University professor Ibram X. Kendi, whose works on "anti-racism" are widely hailed by proponents of critical race theory.[3]

And yet, BLM has been legitimized by a nomination for the Nobel PEACE Prize. I can only conclude there is a form of mass hysteria taking hold in America.

I suggest in our Progressive new world, everything is acceptable. And in the call to please ourselves, to concentrate on our personal rights without mention of responsibility, we have broken trust and loyalty and left our lambs in the fields unprotected.

Here is an excerpt from the International Federation for Family Development (IFFD) NGO in Special Consultative Status with the United Nations Economic and Social Council (ECOSOC): The Crucial Role of Families.

> [W]e can say that sustainable development is not only an economic concept, but it also embraces a profound and fundamental ethical and human dimension. Culture is an important aspect of sustainable development, as it refers

---

2 https://www.blacklivesmatteratschool.com/starter-kit.html

3 Bill Pan, "Schools Embrace BLM 'Week of Action,' Teach Students to 'Disrupt Western Nuclear Family Dynamics,'" *The Epoch Times*, February 2, 2022.

to how we understand and appreciate natural resources and each other. This dimension should be included in the definition of sustainable development, so that it refers to the future generations and the physical environment within the context of the redistribution of culture and wealth, and the eradication of poverty in the world.

And it is from this perspective that I feel families come in, as the environment where ethical and cultural values are achieved in a natural way. As basic and essential building blocks of societies, families have a crucial role in social development. They bear the primary responsibility for the education and socialization of children as well as instilling values of citizenship and belonging in the society. Families provide material and non-material care and support to its members, from children to older persons or those suffering from illness, sheltering them from hardship to the maximum possible extent.[4]

The Bible describes what happens to our family, tribe, and nation when we allow ourselves to follow our own nature rather than agreed upon ethics. The first family had a hellish start: fratricide. Cain killed his own brother. Abraham misled the pharaoh into believing that Sarah was his sister, not his wife, in order to spare his own life. Lot's daughters gave birth to children conceived by their father. Jacob, his mother's favorite, stole Esau's birthright and later was tricked into marrying Leah when he had asked for Rachel. Joseph's brothers threw him into a pit before selling him into slavery; they were jealous of him because he was their father's favorite. These are stories of unbridled human nature. The Bible is a book full of stories that teach us how to be compassionate people in a compassionate society. And it starts with family.

We start in a family, the smallest unit of authority, and come together to form tribes, thus transferring our loyalty to tribal leaders. With time and the development of cities and city-

---

4 International Federation for Family Development, *The Crucial Role of Families*, undated. https://www.un.org/ecosoc/sites/www.un.org.ecosoc/files/files/en/integration/2017/IFFD.pdf.

states and ultimately to countries, loyalty has to move up the chain to the leaders of each new, larger unit. For loyalty to be maintained, there must be commonly shared stories, commonly shared beliefs, desires and goals. In the West, those common shared values come from the Hebrew Bible: the Judeo-Christian ethic—the only ethic that makes a freedom-loving nation possible.

The family creates connections to the past and to the future. Today, many people are looking up their ancestry, revealing a need to connect beyond one's self. At the same time, we are witnessing a full-frontal attack on the nuclear family. To what end, other than to destroy authority from the bottom up as "wokeness" and progressive policies destroy it from the top down?

> [Karl] Marx also despised the nuclear family, which he claimed "performs ideological functions for Capitalism" and teaches "passive acceptance of hierarchy." He thought that the destruction of the family model would make it easier to abolish private property.[5]

Mark Tapson writes of Marx and the family:

> It is 'the abolition of the family,' as Karl Marx explicitly put it, that is central to the success of the communist agenda. As the most fundamental bond of humanity, it is the most resistant bulwark against totalitarian state control and a collectivist mindset. It is the environment in which we are first civilized and molded, ideally, into productive citizens who value our individualism but embrace our role in the larger society. As Edmund Burke wrote in 1790, the family "is the first link in the series by which we proceed towards a love to our country, and to mankind." The all-powerful state to which communists demand allegiance is not a link in that chain, and thus the family is an obstacle that must be dismantled. This is not a conspiracy theory; it is explicitly stated in communist and feminist theory.
> (...)

---

5 Larry Sand, "Child Abuse in Plain Sight," *American Greatness*, April 14, 2021.

This Marxist imperative – to decouple children from their parents and absorb them into the collective – directly echoes a statement from contemporary Progressive Melissa Harris-Perry, an MSNBC host … declared in a 2013 network promo, 'We have to break through our kind of private idea that kids belong to their parents or kids belong to their families, and recognize that kids belong to whole communities.'[6]

It is no secret that families have evolved over time; however, all of this change does not mean that the family is a dying institution. About 90 percent of Americans still marry and have children, and those who divorce usually remarry. Though marriages today differ from those of an earlier time, at least in the near future, it appears that marriage will remain a prominent family structure and cultural force. Or at least we can hope.

The International Federation for Family Development (IFFD) has shared its views on the importance of family.

> Taking into account the broad experience of our Federation in dealing with families worldwide, we see every day that family is where the vast majority of people learn the fundamental skills for life, and other institutions confirm it. At the most fundamental level, family structure and family process matters: evidence shows that outcomes for both children and adults are not equal regardless of family background, and public policy should reflect this. Children growing up in healthy, married, two-parent families are more likely to lead happy, healthy and successful lives than those who have not experienced the same level of family security and stability.

> Those who build stable families have a higher life expectancy, lower risks of mental illness, alcoholism and domestic violence. The children show lower infant mortality rate, lower risk drug addiction, and lower incidences of engaging in criminal activities after puberty, higher aca-

---

6 Mark Tapson, "The Road to Civilizational Collapse," *Mark Tapson's blog*, September 30, 2021.

demic achievements, lower incidence of mental illnesses and fewer teenage unwanted pregnancies. A stable family is the lowest cost option for both its members and the State. Furthermore, members of stable families are more disciplined when it comes to fulfilling legal and social norms, contributing towards financing social security.

Families have an "irreplaceable social role." Adults and children today are increasingly faced with obstacles not only to their material but also to their emotional well-being. They often have to cope with families that are dysfunctional, broken through abuse, separation or divorce or fatherless. This is especially true in the least advantaged sections of society and for the weakest members of them, namely, the elderly, women, the indebted and children.

This doesn't mean that families could or should be replaced in their role. On the contrary, they should be helped and empowered in every possible way.[7]

We, in America and Canada in particular, are at another crossroads. In our desire to bring equality to all, we are throwing out the traditional family. The family, where one parent, usually the mother, stayed home to raise the children, instilling them with the values of that family, those parents. Raising children was once an important job. Certainly more important than making widgets, perhaps because one can recall a defective widget.

It is just and right that all people are provided equal opportunity. What happened to the rights of women who want to be mothers? They seem to have been taken away in the name of women's rights. We unintentionally threw away choice. Yes, that is what I said. Choice. How many women today can choose to stay home? Very few. In an attempt to "elevate" women from their traditional roles, we demeaned parenting. When I was at the park with my three children under four, one in the stroller,

---

7 International Federation for Family Development, *The Crucial Role of Families*, undated. https://www.un.org/ecosoc/sites/www.un.org.ecosoc/files/files/en/integration/2017/IFFD.pdf.

one standing on the back of the stroller and one holding my hand, another woman looked at me and my children and asked if I worked. This was in the mid 1970s.

Family values, the term itself, is attacked. It smells of…religion. Remember President Obama calling out Americans who hold on to their guns and religion? How dare you, he seemed to be saying. Yet, the family is the smallest unit of authority in a community, a society. When it breaks down, there is a terrible ripple effect. We have witnessed the effect of fatherless families. What about families whose parents are absent because both need to work to pay the bills?

Warnings have been raised, but largely ignored, as they went against the politically correct assertion that women need to work outside the home, and that children do well in day care.

> In just 25 years, American families have been radically re-structured as the number of women in the workforce has nearly doubled. Instead of parents providing early child care, it is outsourced to virtual strangers. An estimated 12 million American infants, toddlers and preschoolers—more than half of children in this age group—attend day care. The majority of these kids spend close to 40 hours per week in day care; many start when they are only weeks old.
> (…)
> They show that kids who spend long hours in day care have behavior problems that persist well into elementary school. About 26 percent of children who spend more than 45 hours per week in day care go on to have serious behavior problems at kindergarten age. In contrast, only 10 percent of kids who spend less than 10 hours per week have equivalent problems.
> (…)
> Few parents have heard about the National Institute of Child Health and Human Development (NICHD) Study of Early Child Care, an ongoing $100 million survey of 1,100 children. It's the largest and most rigorous examination of day care in history, taking into account family income and the quality of day care. Evidence from the study

shows that the total number of hours a child is without a parent, from birth through preschool, matters. The more time in child care of any kind or quality, the more aggressive the child, according to results published in Child Development. Children in full-time day care were close to three times more likely to show behavior problems than those cared for by their mothers at home.[8]

Morals, values, ethics and laws were established to protect the nuclear family—those against incest, adultery, and laws specifically designed to protect children. Now, out of nowhere, the nuclear family is under attack by Black Lives Matter. Why?

We *know* that a family is the most important social group to lift people out of poverty, yet BLM wants to disrupt, displace, or move away from the two-parent family, despite the fact that married couples are critical to what is called the "success sequence." This attack is an example of malignant normality.

According to the success sequence, shared by Ron Haskins and Isabel Sawhill in their book, *Creating an Opportunity Society*,[9] individuals who get at least a high school diploma, work, and then marry before having any children, in that order, are not likely to be poor in adulthood.[10] Marriage before children is the key. Sadly, too many black children are born to unwed mothers, an astonishing 72 percent (nearly three out of four), compared to 29 percent of whites and 53 percent of Hispanics.[11]

As Wendy Wang and Brad Wilcox observe in their Millennial Success Sequence:

> 97% of Millennials who follow what has been called the 'success sequence'—that is, who get at least a high school

---

8 Heide Lang, "The Trouble With Day Care," *Psychology Today*, May 1, 2005.

9 Ron Haskins and Isabel Sawhill, *Creating an Opportunity Society*, Brookings Institution Press, 2009.

10 See: Bryan Caplan, "What Does the Success Sequence Mean?" *Institute for Family Studies*, February 25, 2021.

11 Jesse Washington, "Blacks struggle with 72 percent unwed mothers rate," *NBC News*, November 7, 2010.

degree, work, and then marry before having any children, in that order—are not poor by the time they reach their prime young adult years (ages 28-34)... after controlling for a range of background factors, the order of marriage and parenthood in Millennials' lives is significantly associated with their financial well-being in the prime of young adulthood. Simply put, compared with the path of having a baby first, marrying before children more than doubles young adults' odds of being in the middle or top income. Meanwhile, putting marriage first reduces the odds of young adults being in poverty by 60% (vs. having a baby first)."[12] What must not be lost in this discussion is Single parenthood makes it very hard to work full-time.[13]

This must not be viewed as the "blame game"—blaming people for their poor decisions, as we are all the product of our culture—what we experience in the community around us. Wang and Wilcox note: "Most men and women have the capacity to make choices, to embrace virtues or avoid vices, and to otherwise take steps that increase or decrease their odds of doing well in school, finding and keeping a job, or deciding when to marry and have children."[14]

This brings me back to the teachings of the Judeo-Christian ethic that promote family. Two parents and children born in wedlock.

Somewhere along the Progressive highway, we decided that fathers were not that important in the grand scheme of things. Nevertheless, despite attempts to rid the world of biology and science—that a man can become a woman and a woman can become a man—it still takes the sperm of a male to meet with the ovum of a female to produce a child.

Professor Jason D. Hill, a gay, black man, wrote about

12   Wendy Wang and W. Bradford Wilcox, *The Millennial Success Sequence: Marriage, Kids, and the "Success Sequence" among Young Adults.* American Enterprise Institute. https://www.aei.org/wp-content/uploads/2017/06/IFS-MillennialSuccessSequence-Final.pdf?x88519.

13   Bryan Caplan, "What Does the Success Sequence Mean?," op. cit.

14   Wendy Wang and W. Bradford Wilcox, op. cit.

men: "Today, those identities and drives are under attack. Masculinity and manliness, the twin attributes of patriarchy, are being criminalized along with vitality, exuberance and displays of moral authority in men and young boys by a phalanx of radical feminists, 'woke' progressives, and systemic nihilists. The goal of these forces is to advance a systemic, nihilistic, gynocentric paradigm that has ushered in an era that will destroy not only men, but civilization itself." He also writes about "fatherless boys committing a disproportionate number of crimes and rapes in America and across the globe, and the need for society to be radically redesigned along traditional gender roles. This is, fundamentally, because men's natural role to lead with moral authority — rooted in their biological natures — has been usurped in the name of egalitarianism and equity."[15]

The court system we have today is aiding and abetting in that destruction—not only of the identity of the man, but his importance in the family and to his children. In the court system, discrimination against men is endemic. Separation, divorce and the default position is Daddy gets every other weekend and every Wednesday. Getting more time requires lots of work and money. And a great deal of heartache for the fathers and their children.

Fathers are important to girls, as well. As Jordan Peterson has written:

> What kind of families produce violent young men? Fatherless families. The pernicious effect of fatherlessness is exceptionally well-documented. No serious researchers question it. Even the generally damnable sociologists admit it (see, for example, here https://www.ncbi.nlm.nih.gov/pmc/articles/PMC3904543/). Fatherless girls tend toward early sexual experimentation (something in itself linked to antisocial behavior) and, unsurprisingly, higher rates of teenage pregnancy. What might be more surprising, however, is that there is even evidence for earlier puberty among girls whose fathers are absent. Fa-

---

15 Jason D. Hill, "Ethical Patriarchy: Our Final Hope for Western Civilization?" *FrontPage Magazine*, March 31, 2021.

therless boys are over-represented as alcoholics, addicts, gang-members, prisoners, rapists and murderers.

If it is fatherless boys who are violent, how can it be that masculine socialization produces harm both to mental health and society? The data should indicate precisely the opposite: that boys who are only raised by women are much less violent than boys who have men in their lives and, similarly, that boys who do have fathers are more violent than those who do not.

This is not the case. Period.[16]

---

16 Jordan Peterson, "It's ideology vs. science in psychology's war on boys and men," *National Post*, February 1, 2019.

17

Divorce and Destruction of the Family

WHEN TWO PEOPLE divorce, it is more than a marriage that ends. It is the death of a dream for which the seed was planted many years before. Friends remind me that in my second year at university, I said that I wanted to get married and have children. Those were my priorities: to be a good wife and mother. The dream included walking down the aisle together, holding newborn children, and eventually, grandchildren, living long enough to watch our grandchildren get married, and, with the grace of God, to live long enough to hold a great-grandchild in our arms together. For those who divorce, that dream is gone.

The end of a marriage can destroy all those dreams, and for many families there is anger in the ashes of litigation. Anger prevents logical thinking. It can destroy whatever respect remained before the separation. We forget that mother and father, though no longer husband and wife, are together for all eternity in the DNA of their children, their grandchildren and all those who come after.

We have, as a society, experimented in family construction since the early 1970s, when the attacks on the biological family began. The paradigm shifted from the importance of an intact family to the importance of the happiness and self-fulfillment of the parents, the adults. We were told that children are resilient and that it is better for them to live with a happy parent than in a household that was stressful.

In 1859, John Stuart Mill called for "experiments in living" so that we might learn from one another. "As it is useful that while mankind are imperfect there should be different opinions, so is it that there should be different experiments of living; that free scope should be given to varieties of character, short of injury to others; and that the worth of different modes of life should be proved practically, when anyone thinks fit to try them."[1]

The time has come to appraise the results of those experiments.

In America today, between 40-50 percent of marriages end in divorce.[2] And, approximately 30 percent of America's families with children under 18 years old, amounting to 10 million households, are single-parent families. The share of American families with children living with a single parent has tripled since 1965. The large majority of those single-parent families, approximately 75 percent, are headed by a mother only. Sadly, while 21 percent of white children live in a single-parent family, the proportion increases to 28 percent of Hispanic children and is 51 percent of Black children. Over the past half century, the percentages have increased rapidly, tripling for white children, more than doubling for Black and increasing by one-third for Hispanic children.[3]

> Research has documented that parental divorce/separation is associated with an increased risk for child and adolescent adjustment problems, including academic difficulties (e.g., lower grades and school dropout), disruptive behaviors (e.g., conduct and substance use problems), and depressed mood.[4]

---

1   John Stuart Mill, *On Liberty,* Chapter III, 1859.

2   "48 Divorce Statistics Including Divorce Rate, Race, & Marriage Length," *It's Over Easy*, April 19, 2021.

3   Joseph Chamie, "America's single-parent families," *The Hill*, March 19, 2021.

4   Brian D'Onofrio and Robert Emery, "Parental divorce or separation and children's mental health," *National Library of Medicine*, January 2, 2019.

The conclusion to be drawn from these statistics:

> It is widely recognized that children in two parent families fare better in many ways, including in school, personal relationships, social behavior, careers and employment than children with only one parent at home.[5]

Christianity promised monogamy and security to women. Two shall become as one. Till death do you part. Let no man put asunder what God has consecrated. Muslims can divorce with nine words: I divorce thee, I divorce thee, I divorce thee. Native Canadian women suffer horribly with divorce. They can end up with nothing. In Judaism, marriage is considered a contract with mutual rights and obligations that can be ended by mutual consent—a divorce. Not always pleasant.

Marriage brings together two people who hopefully will form a family. The family is the smallest unit of authority in a society. It is an economic engine. It is the source of morals, values and ethics. Healthy societies need healthy, intact families. I remember hearing from therapists in the late 1960s and early '70s, that it was better to divorce than have children live in a state of tension.

Living is a state of tension. We all have to learn to live with anxiety as human beings because we are constantly called upon to choose because we have the gift of free will. A gift that has evolved over the millennia and is held sacrosanct in a democracy. A gift that comes in two parts—rights and responsibilities.

I can understand ending a marriage when there is abuse. It is not safe to raise a child in a home that is full of fear, fear that a parent or child will be hurt, fear there will be no food on the table, or no table, no roof, because a parent has an addiction that eats all of the income. There are very good reasons for divorce.

Although there are times when a divorce is the best solution, there are unfortunately some very bad reasons to end a marriage. What is a most interesting statistic is that more than

---

5 Joseph Chamie, op. cit.

half of all divorces occur in low-conflict marriages. They are referred to as "good enough" marriages, ones that could be saved. In one study, 64% of couples who said they were unhappy but stayed together and worked on their relationship said they were happy five years later.[6] That may sound like a long time, but those five years spent working it out adds five more years to your children's security. Divorces that take place in low-conflict marriages can be very damaging to children.

Divorcing parents often forget that their children have rights. A child's right to security must always trump an adult's desire for more zing in her relationship. And don't fool yourself into thinking that older kids will understand. They won't. Their security is destroyed no matter how old they are. I remember one of my twenty-something children saying, "I don't like the fact that I have to call two parents to share news." So small a detail—so big a hurt.

John Stuart Mill took into account that people are entitled to act on their own opinions "without hindrance, either physical or moral, from their fellow-men" so long as it was "at their own risk and peril." He noted this last proviso was "of course indispensable." He insisted that: "When … a person is led to violate a distinct and assignable obligation to any other person or persons, the case is taken out of the self-regarding class, and becomes amenable to moral disapprobation in the proper sense of the term." Can anyone name any action taken by anyone that does not affect others?

Mature, responsible adults know that after children come into a marriage, life is no longer self-regarding, about their own happiness. It is about their children. I remember my late Aunt Lil used to say, "Everyone wants to be happy, happy, happy. What is wrong with one happy at a time?" Children, if given the opportunity to speak openly and honestly will tell you that it isn't enough to see daddy only on Wednesday and every other weekend. As physical custody tends to rest with the mother, children, especially boys, suffer from a father deficit. And that

6 See: Harry Benson, "Should Couples in Unhappy Marriages Stay Together?," *Institute for Family Studies*, February 22, 2017.

is not healthy for the child or society. Children suffer emotionally having to divide holidays between parents. Or divide life between two households. Or divide loyalty between parents. Or live in fear of telling a parent the truth about where they want to live. Divorce affects relationships with the extended family. Grandparents tend to be forgotten in all of this. Many lose access to their grandchildren. Children have a richer life when exposed to grandparents and the larger extended family.

Professor Ronald Rohner, professor emeritus of family studies at the University of Connecticut, and co-author of a study that appeared in the May 2012 *Personality and Social Psychology Review,* wrote: "There's a very consistent worldwide effect of impaired psychologically adjustment wherever kids perceive themselves to be rejected by Mom or Dad. And the effect shows up more significantly for dads than their moms." He added, "In our 50 years of research in every continent but Antarctica, we have found that nothing has as strong and consistent an effect in personality as does being rejected by a parent especially a father." And after analyzing 36 international studies from 18 countries that took place between 1975 and 2010 that included 1,400 parents between 18 and 89 years, and 8,600 children from 9-18 years, all concluded that the need for a father in a child's life is one of the most important factors in developing healthy children, emotionally. Rohner noted: "Our work should encourage dads to really get involved in the loving care of their children at an early age. Their kids will be measurably better off."[7]

Most importantly, the financial security of a fatherless child drops, in some cases precipitously. It is true that material things should not be idolized, but children are the first to suffer when two households are needed and both parents must go to work. The children from these divorces will now have less time to spend with both parents and more time in child care. Children living in one-parent households are twice as likely to be at the bottom 40% of household income compared to children

7 "Dad's Love Can Be Crucial for Happy Childhood, Study Confirms," *HealthDay News,* June 15, 2012.

living with two parents.[8] Less money, less opportunity.

8   Rebecca O'Neill, "Experiments in Living: The Fatherless Family," *Civitas*, September 2002.

18

Mental Illness, Divorce and Fatherless Children

FATHERLESS HOMES account for 90% of homeless children, 85% of childhood behavioral problems, 71% of high school dropouts, 63% of youth suicides, 50% of teen mothers, and 85% of incarcerated youth.[1] Separation from a parent can be a major challenge for some children and result in problems lasting a lifetime.

> Empirical and academic evidence has documented that parental divorce or separation causes many adjustment problems for child and adolescent. The problems include depressed mood, academic difficulties (e.g., lower grades and school dropout), and disruptive behaviors (e.g., conduct and substance use problems).
>
> (...)
>
> [E]ven before marital breakup, children whose parents later divorce exhibit higher levels of anxiety/depression and antisocial behavior than children whose parents remain married. There is a further increase in child anxiety/depression associated with the event of parental divorce itself.

---

1 "The Importance of Father Daughter Relationships," *All4kids.org*, June 12, 2019. https://www.all4kids.org/news/blog/the-importance-of-father-daughter-relationships/.

The adverse effects of divorce on mental health may stay with child/adolescent well into their adulthood. In another study of 17,414 individuals in UK who were followed from ages 7 to 33, researchers found that experiencing parental divorce during childhood was related to worse mental health when the offspring were in their 20s and 30s.[2]

Absent Fathers

Children do not ask to be born. Children are the result of a male sperm meeting up with a female ovum and a baby is created. A man and a woman make a baby. This used to be known by all, often learned by children from their friends sharing their "knowledge" in the schoolyard.

Children need fathers. And we know this for a fact because of the positive effects on our children. Studies show that school-aged children with good relationships with their fathers were less likely to experience depression, to exhibit disruptive behavior, or to lie. Overall, they were far more likely to exhibit prosocial behavior. Research shows definitively that children do better when fathers are present.

> Even from birth, children who have an involved father are more likely to be emotionally secure, be confident to explore their surroundings, and, as they grow older, have better social connections.
> (...)
> Children with involved, caring fathers have better educational outcomes…Numerous studies find that an active and nurturing style of fathering is associated with better verbal skills, intellectual functioning, and academic achievement among adolescents.[3]

---

2 "Effects of Divorce on Children's Mental Health," *GenPsych.org*, October 17, 2020.

3 "Fathers and Their Impact on Children's Well-Being," Parentcentre.org, undated. https://theparentcentre.org.za/fathers-and-their-impact-on-children's-well-being/.

Furthermore:

Father involvement is related to positive child health outcomes in infants, such as improved weight gain in preterm infants and improved breastfeeding rates.

Father involvement using authoritative parenting (loving and with clear boundaries and expectations) leads to better emotional, academic, social, and behavioral outcomes for children.

Children who feel a closeness to their father are: twice as likely as those who do not to enter college or find stable employment after high school, 75% less likely to have a teen birth, 80% less likely to spend time in jail, and half as likely to experience multiple depression symptoms.

Fathers occupy a critical role in child development. Father absence hinders development from early infancy through childhood and into adulthood. The psychological harm of father absence experienced during childhood persists throughout the life course.
(...)
High levels of father involvement are correlated with higher levels of sociability, confidence, and self-control in children. Children with involved fathers are less likely to act out in school or engage in risky behaviors in adolescence.
(...)
Children with actively involved fathers are: 43% more likely to earn A's in school and 33% less likely to repeat a grade than those without engaged dads.
(...)
Father engagement reduces the frequency of behavioral problems in boys while also decreasing delinquency and economic disadvantage in low-income families.

Father engagement reduces psychological problems and rates of depression in young women.
(...)
[C]hildren consistently report feeling abandoned when

their fathers are not involved in their lives, struggling with their emotions and episodic bouts of self-loathing.
(...)
Mental health disorders (father absent children are consistently overrepresented on a wide range of mental health problems, particularly anxiety, depression and suicide).

According to the U.S. Census Bureau 2020, 18.3 million children, 1 in 4, live without a biological, step, or adoptive father in the home.[4]

Let's talk about fathers and daughters.

Fathers are just as important in the lives of their daughters as their sons. If a daughter has a good relationship with her father, she has a lower risk of developing anxiety or depression and she deals with stress better. These daughters are also less likely to develop eating disorders, body dysmorphia, or be dissatisfied with their appearance or body weight. Dad is the first "beau," and if a dad works on developing a close bond with his daughter and makes it comfortable for her to talk about her feelings, he sets her up for successful and fulfilling relationships in the future. A loving, caring dad helps a daughter to develop self-confidence and create a positive self-image.[5]

According to the Institute for Family Studies, a girl who has a strong relationship with her father is less likely to experience a teen pregnancy and far less likely to become sexually active in her early teens and have more satisfying, long-lasting marriages.[6] And this is so important in today's culture where girls are online, often alone in their rooms, affected by "influencers," who may not have your family's values.

Fatherlessness is the single greatest predictor of criminal

---

4 See: "A Father's Impact on Child Development," *All4Kids.org*, June 7, 2018. https://www.all4kids.org/news/blog/a-fathers-impact-on-child-development/.

5 See: "Scientists Claim Fathers Have a Bigger Impact on Daughters' Lives, and We're Curious to Learn Why," *Brightside*, undated.

6 "The Importance of Father Daughter Relationships," *All4kids.org*, June 12, 2019.

activity in boys and promiscuity in girls. A child in a father-absent home is more likely to live in poverty, more likely to suffer from obesity and addiction, twice as likely to drop out of high school and is more likely to face abuse and neglect from an unrelated man in the home.

Progressive attacks on the family are harming children of colour the most. The murder rate amongst black boys should make us wonder why this has not been declared a public emergency by those very same Progressives-who-care.

From Larry Elder:

> Nearly 70 percent of black kids are born to unwed mothers. The dropout rate in some urban high schools approaches 50 percent. Of those who do graduate, many cannot read or do math at a 12th-grade level.

> The No. 1 cause of preventable death for young white men is accidents, such as car accidents. The No. 1 cause of preventable death for young black men is homicide, almost always committed by other young black men. In Chicago, a city approximately one-third white, one-third black and one-third Hispanic, blacks accounted for nearly 80 percent of homicide victims in 2018, and most of these cases remain unsolved. According to a 2017 report by the Centers for Disease Control, a black child is almost 10 times more likely to be a victim of a gun-related homicide than a white child.[7]

We won't call it a public emergency, because we don't want to hurt anyone's feelings. Like single mothers—especially single minority mothers—because that would be racist. Feelings are so much more important than lives.

And we know the importance of fathers because of the damage done when a father is not present. With all of this information, all of this experience, why would any group promote dismantling the traditional family?

---

7 Larry Elder, "The Virginia Blackface Follies," *Jewish World Review*, February 14, 2019.

19

Transgender and the Breakdown of Family

One man, one woman, and children.

I N THE BIBLE, it says in Gen. 1:27: *And God created man in His image; in the image of God He created him; male and female He created them.* Male and female.

Now, I am not one to turn to the Bible for science, but for the past 3500 years, we have been taught that there are two sexes—male and female. We got along quite well with that statement and surprise! It has been shared by the scientific community for a very long time. Before this century, I doubt anyone had thought of dividing humanity into multiple sexes and genders. Perhaps because humanity was busy with real science and real life and didn't have time to mull the ridiculous.

And "Therefore a man shall leave his father and his mother and hold fast to his wife, and they shall become one flesh." —Genesis 2:24.

Remarkable how this has worked for the past 3500 years and tens of thousands before that. But all that has changed.

There are people on social media, known as influencers, who reach out to your children and teach them about sex. These influencers are reaching your children at a tender, impressionable age, confusing them and pushing them to believe that it is terrific to mutilate their bodies. They enter your children's room, when you are not there, to seduce them. Meet just a few:

Alex Bertie is a Transgender man who not only runs an amazing Youtube Channel with 309K subscribers but is also an author of the book *Trans Mission: My Quest To A Beard.*

Nikita Dragun is a social media star, model, makeup artist, fashion entrepreneur, beauty guru and trans-right activist. She first rose to fame from her highly popular You-Tube channel when she posted an emotional video tagged "I am transgender", which has since gone viral. Her You-Tube currently has 1.8 million subscribers and she uses her platform to advocate for Trans Rights, authenticity, acceptance and inclusivity.

Jazz Jennings is the 18-year-old star of TLC's reality show "I Am Jazz." She began living as her authentic self at age 5 (because at 5 you know who you are), and with the aid of her parents, she asserted her identity as a girl while demanding her school treat her as one. Jennings has since ascended into a role as one of the nation's foremost trans activists and social media influencers. Her YouTube channel has more than 560k subscribers and offers a personal account about her transitioning journey and the experiences she has along the way.

Kai Wes Bigwood is a transmaculine nonbinary hero. Using their Instagram platform to document their top surgery and transition, Bigwood advocates for trans-awareness and anti-LGBT+ bullying. They have a shock of coiffed blonde hair, regularly rock beanies and backwards caps, and frequently post photos of themselves shirtless, embracing their post-op chest. Candid and honest, Bigwood shows us how queer and lovely life can be.

Eli Erlick is a gender non-conforming trans woman who's here, queer, and dapper beyond words. As a gender non-conforming trans woman, Erlick is constantly questioned on her more masculine presenting appearance but combats it with genuine activism coupled with personal anecdotes.

Coming out as transgender at age 4, Avery Jackson was supported by her parents to fully transition, and through this experience she has become an advocate for LGBT youth. Her story made national headlines as her parents were passionate about going to great lengths to help their daughter be happy. Combatting the lack of representation of transgender children, Avery has helped other families find strength and encouragement in their own trans journeys.[1]

Social media is making it too easy for others to teach YOUR children, to infect them with dangerous propaganda, anathema to your values.

Let me now introduce you to Drag Queen Story Hour performers Fay and Fluffy who have read at the Toronto Public Libraries, Art Gallery of Ontario, The Royal Ontario Museum and to classrooms across Ontario.[2] For those unfamiliar with Toronto, Canada, it is Canada's largest city and the world's most diverse city. Fluffy is very obviously a man dressed as a woman. He has a hairy chest, a beard, wears a dress and a great big bright yellow wig. Fay and Fluffy were very upset when their appearances were questioned by Meghan Murphy (more about Meghan, later) who shared her concern about the danger of "self-identification" as the standard for gender-based human rights protection.

Among the "controversial" things Ms. Murphy said was, "On what basis do women's rights exist if the word 'woman' is meaningless?"[3]

---

1   "13 Trans Influencers & Activists That Inspire Us," *Teen Line*, December 12, 2018.

2   Nico Johnson, "Drag queens, Fay and Fluffy, cut ties with Toronto Library over Murphy talk," *Post Millenial*, October 30, 2019.

3   Chris Selley, "Attack on public libraries for letting Meghan Murphy speak is a nauseating spectacle," *National Post*, October 30, 2019.

Fay and Fluffy announced they would henceforth boycott Toronto Public Libraries, because it let someone rent a room and invite Meghan Murphy to speak her truth.

> Kaleb Robertson, who is the "Fluffy" of the duo, stated on Instagram that they could not "continue a relationship with a space that will host someone who is actively fighting to take away my legal rights as a human."
> (...)
> The duo stated that "Trans people existing and having rights to employment, housing, and safety is not a discussion."[4]

These are the people who want to read to your children in the library and in school. Young children. Why should we share this with pre-pubescent children? What is the purpose? These children barely know the science of sex and making babies but let's confuse them with belief?

And then we have PBS. When my children were growing up, we watched PBS for their amazing shows for children. *Sesame Street* was truly revolutionary back then. But, today, something has gone askew. Mark Tapson writes:

> In 2021 PBS aired a children's show, produced in partnership with the New York City Department of Education, called Let's Learn, featuring a man in drag going by the alias "Little Miss Hot Mess," singing, dancing, and reading his book about drag queens to an intended audience of three to eight-year-olds. Little Miss Hot Mess is one of the founding members of Drag Queen Story Hour in public libraries across the country, in which garishly-costumed men posing as grotesque parodies of women normalize gender confusion and groom unsuspecting children while their naïve, woke moms stand by feeling virtuous.[5]

---

4   Nico Johnson, "Drag queens, Fay and Fluffy, cut ties with Toronto Library over Murphy talk," *Post Millenial*, October 30, 2019.

5   Mark Tapson, "The Road to Civilizational Collapse," *Mark Tapson's blog*, September 30, 2021.

Wait, there's more!

> The National Sex Education Standards, which provided
> a roadmap for Nebraska Department of Education, teach
> kindergartners the names of reproductive body parts
> and define gender identity and reproduction. Children
> in Grades 3-5 are taught about masturbation, hormone
> blockers used to transition pre-pubescent children, STDs,
> and the differences between cisgender, transgender, non-
> binary, and "gender expansive." Grades 6-8 are taught
> about abortion, contraception, and differences between
> vaginal, oral, and anal sex. Grades 9-10 must teach 'repro-
> ductive justice,' which entails unlimited abortion access.
> (...)
> Advocates for Youth[6] was founded in 1980 and focuses on
> improving 'youth sexual health and rights,' according to
> its website. The CDC has given Advocates for Youth $26
> million in grants since 1995, with an additional $3.8 mil-
> lion coming from Health and Human Services, according
> to TAGGS. The group boasts that it distributes millions
> of condoms to students every year. Its YouTube show, Ki-
> kis with Louie, promotes topics such as transgenderism,
> gender fluidity, and drag queens to children. One of the
> groups youth activism programs, titled "Abortion Out
> Loud," aims to "end abortion stigma and strengthen sup-
> port for young people's access to abortion."[7]

Abortion stigma? Have we gone mad? This is not about
the right or wrong of abortion. This is about a culture that cele-
brates the taking of life.

And more from Mark Tapson, Shillman Fellow on Popular Culture for the David Horowitz Freedom Center:

> In Illinois, legislators passed a bill requiring K-12 public
> schools that offer sex education to align their curriculum
> with the National Sex Education Standards (NSES). These
> standards state that between grades K-2 children should

---

6 See their website here: https://www.3rs.org/.

7 Patrick Hauf, "Meet the CDC-Backed Groups That Want To Teach Trans
Ideology to Kindergartners," *Washington Free Beacon*, July 24, 2021.

learn to "define gender, gender identity, and gender role stereotypes." Between grades 3-5, children should learn to "distinguish between sex assigned at birth and gender identity," "define and explain differences between cisgender, transgender, gender nonbinary, gender expansive, and gender identity," and "explain that gender expression and gender identity exist along a spectrum." The standards also require that children be taught about "power and privilege, conscious and unconscious bias, intersectionality, and covert and overt discrimination, and the principles of reproductive justice, racial justice, social justice, and equity."[8]

Professor Jason Hill writes:

This is a culture in which postmodern ethical relativism is accepted as the norm in schools, and where students are taught that logic, reason, grammar, science and now math are racist. They are constructs of white imperial racists, students are told. The social justice ideologies of ANTI-FA and Black Lives Matter are being mainstreamed in the K-12 curricula in schools in the United States.[9]

While you were looking the other way, or fearful of being canceled, books like these found their way onto library shelves for your children and grandchildren: *The Hips on the Drag Queen Go Swish, Swish, Swish, Race Cars: A Children's Book About White Privilege* and *How Mommas Love Their Babies* featuring wholesome lines like "Some mommas dance all night long in special shoes. It's hard work!" The illustrations accompanying that page are an outdoor shot of a strip club at night, with glowing neon lights and a woman protesting for fair wages for strippers.[10]

8 Mark Tapson, "The Left's Urgent Mission to Sexualize Children," *Front-Page Magazine*, June 7, 2021.

9 Jason D. Hill, "Ethical Patriarchy: Our Final Hope for Western Civilization?" *FrontPage Magazine*, March 31, 2021.

10 Bethany Mandel, "Saving children's books from wokeness," *American Spectator*, November 20, 2021.

As Bari Weiss said: "There's one word that sums up how we've gotten to this insane impasse, and it's cowardice. The number one ingredient that if it were present would change the outcome of all of these stories…is courage. It's a story of cowardice and courage, the moment that we're in."[11]

This "controversy" should not be about trans people and their feelings. This is about children. Impressionable wee people. We must teach our young people about inclusion. Absolutely. They must be comfortable with people unlike themselves—different races, colours, absolutely. And just as importantly, people with physical and mental disabilities. They must be able to comfortably talk to people in wheelchairs, or those who are missing limbs, or those who are deaf or blind. They must be comfortable talking to people who have a difficult time understanding the world. When they go out into the world, these are the people they will meet and with whom they will interact. But the possibility of the majority of our children interacting with someone like Fluffy is at best, negligible. After they grow up, if they decide this is the milieu they want, they can find it.

There was a time when drag queens performed for adults. Men dressing up and acting as women has a long history. It was pretend:

> Dressing in drag was once just a means of fulfilling female parts in plays — and now it's become a worldwide phenomenon.

> Drag as an art form has exploded largely thanks to the life and career of RuPaul, Andre Charles — arguably the most famous drag queen in the world today.

> [T]he history of drag as a form of entertainment dates back to Shakespearean times and for more utilitarian purposes. Indeed, the history of drag seems to be one inextricably tied to the theatre, and before the theatre of Shakespeare's time, the stage was used for religious purposes.

---

11 Ibid.

> [I]n the 17th century when Shakespeare's plays were first performed at the Globe Theatre in London, only men were allowed to take part in the productions, as they were in religious rites. So when plays included female parts, the male actors would dress as women to fill the void.
>
> (...)
>
> Female impersonation and the history of drag is said to have entwined with gay culture around the 1930's.[12]

Do you think any of the performers looked like Fay or Fluffy? By the 1990s, the world was ready to make the drag queen more mainstream than ever before.

> RuPaul Charles changed the history of drag in the modern age.
>
> (...)
>
> RuPaul, who soon after became the first drag queen to ever become a spokesperson for a major cosmetics company with MAC Cosmetics, got his own talk show on VH1, and a morning radio show on WKTU.[13]

Perhaps in the name of feminism and women, we should have strippers and prostitutes come and speak. After all, what girl does not grow up wishing to be a "sex worker" so she can be sexually abused for money? And what girl does not want to be a stripper? And if she hasn't yet thought about it by age ten...?

How did we get to a place where language separated women from their biological reality? How did we arrive at "menstruators, birthing people, pregnant people, lactating people, chestfeeders?" We've entered a world where schoolteachers are telling parents not to "gender" their children and who are telling their students not to use words such as "Mom" and "Dad."

> According to the American Psychological Association, the terms "natal sex" and "birth sex," for example, are now

---

12 Bernadette Deron, "The Evolution Of The Art Of Drag In 33 Stunning, Historical Images," *All That's Interesting*, December 15, 2018.

13 Ibid., See also: Ryan Roschke, "Sashay Through the History of Drag Queen Culture," *PopSugar*, September 5, 2019.

considered "disparaging"; the preferred term is "assigned sex at birth." The National Institutes of Health, the CDC, and Harvard Medical School have all made efforts to divorce sex from medicine and emphasize gender identity.[14]

We inhabit a country of multiple trans movements that are encouraging gender reassignments on children as young as eight years old and prescribing puberty blockers for pre-teens. In this world, people can be fired from their jobs for "misgendering" a person.

Here are a few excerpts from writer/journalist Katie Herzog's ongoing series about the spread of woke ideology in the field of medicine.

> "{A}cknowledging biological sex can be considered transphobic."
> (...)
> In a lecture on transgender health, an instructor declared: "Biological sex, sexual orientation, and gender are all constructs. These are all constructs that we have created."
> (...)
> Her medical school hosts an online forum in which students correct their instructors for using terms like "male" and "female" or "breastfeed" instead of "chestfeed."
> (...)
> Then there are the petitions. At the beginning of the year, students circulate a number of petitions designed to "name and shame" instructors for "wrongspeak."[15]

Who wants one of these people as a doctor? They can't, or mustn't, tell a male from a female? Men and women are different!

> "One of the biggest things we've learned is that cellular biology is sex-specific," says Sarah L. Berga, MD, Wake Forest Baptist Health's chair of obstetrics and gynecology

---

14 Katie Herzog, "Med Schools Are Now Denying Biological Sex," *Common Sense* Bari Weiss' Substack account, July 27, 2021.

15 Ibid.

and vice president for women's health services. "When we look closely, we tend to find differences between men and women" and "Every single cell has a chromosomal sex, and the 'cellular machinery' is independent of hormones."

"But we've also learned that most sex differences are the result of the interaction between this chromosomal distinction and hormones."

As a result, it is now commonly accepted that there is a biological basis for sex differences in a number of common conditions, among them heart disease, stroke, arthritis, dementia, colon cancer and depression. And there's active research into why other conditions—including obesity, bronchitis, asthma, multiple sclerosis and thyroid disease—occur more frequently in women than men.

"We're beginning to truly understand how men and women differ in very fundamental ways and how these differences affect disease risk, symptoms, diagnostic sensitivity and specificity, and responses to therapy," says Berga, who joined the Wake Forest Baptist faculty in November 2011. "We now need to adjust our approaches and develop sex-specific interventions and therapies so both men and women benefit."

The best way to do that, she says, is through research that directly compares men and women.[16]

How did we ever know about sex before language and books? How was it possible for our ancestors to raise children not knowing their sex? To think that for thousands upon thousands of years we knew boys from girls by looking at them—a boy has a penis, yes I said penis, and a girl has a vagina. We know just by looking. Yet, today, it seems our eyes deceive us. Now you cannot tell a boy from a girl anymore by looking. Oh

---

16 "Medicine Looking Deeper Into Vital Differences Between Women and Men," *Wake Forest Baptist*, undated. https://www.wakehealth.edu/Stories/ Differences-Between-Men-and-Women.

no. It is now a decision made in the early years by the child. Do you *feel* like a boy or a girl? And, our children are inundated with these lies and bullied into accepting them in kindergarten. Why? To what end, other than the destruction of family, science and sanity and the promotion of cultural relativism? This is malignant normality taking hold. And the parents too often stay silent. What happened to you?

I studied gender in University, when I returned in the 1990s. We learned about sex and gender. Sex is based on chromosomes. XX is female, XY is male. That can never be changed, despite the attempt to deny biology. One cannot be transformed from a female to a male or male to female. I know this is blasphemy. However, there is gender fluidity—from a manly man to a more feminine man, and a feminine woman to a more manly woman. The question we must raise is why is there this call to chemically and surgically try to change sex? A male who "becomes" a female does not have ova. A female who "becomes" a male does not have sperm. What do these people want other than the destruction of family by destroying the creators of family? And then what?

And for all of this talk about transgender from people who say there is no such thing as gender, why are they demanding a female president?

It is Progressive malignant normality that makes all of this possible. And too many parents are remaining silent, too often out of fear of being chastised and bullied. It is time to strip the emperor of his clothing. There is no scientific data that proves a boy can become a girl or a girl can become a boy. We are born into our sex. We do not tell children in kindergarten that they will decide when they are older if they are a boy or girl. It has been decided for 99.9% of all people at birth, when the doctor delivers the baby and looks for the presence or absence of a vagina.

Attacks on Children

These are attacks on the family and on children in particular. What will the long-term damage be to children who are told at a tender age that they are not who they think they are? They are not boys or girls. That there are no absolutes in life?

Today, you are expected to understand that gender is not binary as biological science, your eyes, and your own experience have led you to believe. Whatever you learned about biology growing up is not only wrong, it's pathological and harmful. You no longer know how many genders you're expected to be able to recognize. You *do know* that asking questions is dangerous.

Children are being asked, "What are your pronouns?" What? Do they even know the meaning of pronoun? But asking them simply confuses them about their identity. It's like asking a child to question their race.

We are living in a time of disfigured language being forced on us. New words for a mauled science. An alternate reality. How can anyone ever be expected to learn this language?

Cisgender: Those who identify as the sex they were assigned at birth. For example, a baby born with a vulva is categorized a girl. If she also sees herself as a girl throughout her life, she is considered cisgender. If you don't know the gender of a person, you should call them "they." In 2019, the Merriam-Webster dictionary added "they" as the pronoun to use for a "single person whose gender identity is non-binary." What is non-binary, asked the Beauty? Non-binary gender identity is just one term used to describe individuals who may experience a gender identity that is neither exclusively woman or man or is in between or beyond both genders. Nonbinary individuals may identify as gender fluid, a gender (without gender), genderqueer, or something else entirely. And the sweet Alice felt herself slipping down the rabbit hole. But wait; there is more. Ze is pronounced like "zee" and can also be spelled zie or xe, and replaces she/he/they. Hir is pronounced like "here" and replaces her/hers/him/his/they/theirs.

> Professionals recognize the distress of young people with
> Gender Dysphoria and feel an urge to treat them. At the

same time, most of these professionals have doubts because of the lack of data regarding long-term physical and
psychological outcomes.[17]

Imagine how the children feel. How did we arrive at a
place where we try and change the sex of a person rather than
help them be the sex with which they were born?

January Littlejohn, a licensed mental health counselor,
wonders whether the transgender movement has become a new
source of teenage rebellion. "It's like they're asking to get a nose
ring or their hair dyed or a piece of clothing they know their
parents are going to reject." She also said school policies regarding transgender students "reinforce the confusion they may be
experiencing and affirm in their adolescent brain that they were
born the wrong gender... What we are seeing is absolutely a
social contagion of vulnerable kids, mostly girls."[18]

Are girls falling prey to the phenomenon of collective
suggestion or collective obsessional behaviour or culturally acquired psychosis?

On July 22, 2019, Jerome M. Adams, Surgeon General of
United States Department of Health & Human Services,
had the following to say: "We inform you of a grave public
health concern impacting children and adolescents diagnosed with gender dysphoria. It is an issue so dire that
the Royal College of General Practitioners in the United
Kingdom issued an unprecedented warning to the public
earlier this month."

In the United Kingdom April, 2020:"Minister for Women
and Equalities announced plans to prohibit minors from
undergoing any permanent procedure intended to change
their gender."

---

17 Riittakerttu Kaltiala-Heino, Hannah Bergman, Marja Työläjärvi, and
Louise Frisén, "Gender dysphoria in adolescence: current perspectives,"
National Library of Medicine, March 2, 2018.
18 Patricia Tolson, "Social Media, Schools, and the Secret Rise of Transgender Children: The New 'Social Contagion,'" *The Epoch Times*, August 23,
2021.

A leading U.K. psychiatrist has spoken out against practices that can subject our youth to "serious and irreversible damage."

A study on Transgender health concerns has the following to say: "Hormone therapy is often used to make a transgender person more masculine or feminine. But the use of hormones has risks. Testosterone can damage the liver, especially if taken in high doses. Estrogen can increase blood pressure and blood clotting."[19]

When men take high doses of female hormones, the result can be deadly.

Transgender women on hormone therapy may be at a higher risk for cardiovascular problems, such as stroke, blood clots and heart attack.

The study was done by reviewing eight years of medical records of nearly 5,000 transgender patients in the Kaiser Health system, and looked at patients over the age of 18 who took hormones for gender transition. Over 97,000 cisgender patients — people whose sex assigned at birth matches their gender identity — with similar age and health characteristics were studied for comparison.

This is the largest study of the health of transgender individuals on hormone therapy ever done," said Dr. Darios Getahun, an author of the study and research scientist at Kaiser Permanente. The study found that transgender women, who are assigned the male sex at birth, were twice as likely as cisgender men or women to have the blood clot condition venous thromboembolism. Transgender women on hormone therapy were also found to be 80 to 90 percent more likely to have stroke or a heart attack than cisgender women.[20]

---

19 Brad Salzberg, "Why Media BURY The Dark Side Of 'Transgender Day Of Visibility,'" *Cultural Action Party of Canada Newsletter*, April 1, 2021.

20 Avichai Scher, "Study finds health risks for transgender women on hormone therapy," *NBC News*, July 9, 2018.

Using drugs to stop the onset of puberty is beginning to be questioned.

> The actual science is beginning to overcome transgender ideology. First, the U.K.'s National Institute for Health and Care Excellence — basically the NHS's decision-maker for what to cover — determined that there was "very low" evidence of benefit to allow children with gender dysphoria to have their natural puberty blocked — which is an "off label" use of those drugs.

> Now, Karolinska Hospital, a major health institution in Sweden, is stopping their use. Why? There is little scientific to support such interventions. From the hospital's official statement:

>> In December 2019, the SBU (Swedish Agency for Health Technology Assessment and Assessment of Social Services) published an overview of the knowledge base which showed a lack of evidence for both the long-term consequences of the treatments, and the reasons for the large influx of patients in recent years.

> Even more importantly, the potential for harming the patient physically is very real:

>> These treatments are potentially fraught with extensive and irreversible adverse consequences such as cardiovascular disease, osteoporosis, infertility, increased cancer risk, and thrombosis. This makes it challenging to assess the risk/benefit for the individual patient, and even more challenging for the minors and their guardians to be in a position of an informed stance regarding these treatments.[21]

One of the most comprehensive studies on long-term ef-

---

21 Wesley J. Smith, "Major Swedish Hospital Bans Puberty Blocking for Gender Dysphoria," *National Review*, May 5, 2021. See also: "Policy Change Regarding Hormonal Treatment of Minors with Gender Dysphoria at Tema Barn - Astrid Lindgren Children's Hospital." https://segm.org/sites/default/files/Karolinska%20_Policy_Statement_English.pdf.

fects of transitioning, also performed in Sweden, showed that after surgery, transgender-identifying people were more likely to commit suicide, at a rate 19 times higher than the average population.[22]

> According to the World Professional Association for Transgender Help (WPATH) transgender standards of care, which HHS (Health and Human Services) relies on, "In most children, gender dysphoria will disappear before, or early in puberty." Indeed, WPATH's recommended studies demonstrate that up to 94% of children referred for gender dysphoria (77-94% in one set of studies and 73-88% in another) will grow out of their gender dysphoria naturally.

> Other researchers note that "[e]very study that has been conducted on this has found the same thing. At the moment there is strong evidence that even many children with rather severe gender dysphoria will, in the long run, shed it and come to feel comfortable with the bodies they were born with."[23]

Miriam Grossman, a child and adolescent psychiatrist, writes:

> Increasingly, confused girls with mental-health issues are lining up to have their breasts removed, erroneously believing my colleagues who tell them the operation will alleviate their emotional pain and allow them to emerge as their authentic selves. Girls as young as 13 are having "top surgery," a euphemism for a bilateral mastectomy— the removal of both breasts—in order to create, as gender surgeons put it, a "masculinized" chest. "Bilateral mastectomy" sounds jarring and clinical; it's a treatment for can-

---

22 Cecilia Dhejne, Paul Lichtenstein, Marcus Boman, Anna L. V. Johansson, Niklas Långström, Mikael Landén, "Long-Term Follow-Up of Transsexual Persons Undergoing Sex Reassignment Surgery: Cohort Study in Sweden," *PLOS One*, February 22, 2011.

23 "Summary of Studies Regarding Risks Associated With Transgender Medical Interventions," *HHS Transgender Mandate*, undated. http://www. transgendermandate.org/research.

cer, after all—one that women agonize over."

The Society for Evidence-Based Gender Medicine is arguing against mastectomies for young girls. They point out that long-term outcomes are highly uncertain and that many girls have untreated mental-health issues. They explain why the evidence supporting mastectomies in minors is low-quality and unreliable.

According to SEGM, mastectomies on minors are an "experimental procedure on vulnerable youth" whose brains and identities are still developing. Leading gender clinics and psychiatric associations worldwide are rejecting these procedures. They're saying that girls who want their breasts removed need in-depth psychotherapy, not a surgeon's scalpel.[24]

Here is the story of a woman who had identified as male since the age of 13.

After taking testosterone therapy, her voice deepened, she grew facial hair and her body started to change. She was due to undergo breast-removal surgery this summer, but started to change her mind in May and decided to stop taking her hormones and to identify as female again.

The woman, who asked to be called Ruby says:

"I didn't think any change was going to be enough in the end and I thought it was better to work on changing how I felt about myself, than changing my body. I've seen similarities in the way I experience gender dysphoria, in the way I experience other body image issues."
(...)
"When I was at my gender clinic to get referred for hormones, we had a session where I went over my mental health issues and I told them about my eating disorder and they didn't suggest that that could maybe connected

---

24   Miriam Grossman, "The Moral Atrocity of 'Top Surgery,'" *City Journal.* February 25, 2022.

with my gender dysphoria," she says.

"For everyone who has gender dysphoria, whether they are trans or not, I want there to be more options for us because I think there is a system of saying, 'okay here's your hormones, here's your surgery, off you go.' I don't think that's helpful for anyone."[25]

This reminds me of my mental health care as a senior: "Here's a pill, see you later."

Kenneth Zucker headed up the Family Gender Identity Clinic at The Centre for Addiction and Mental health in Toronto, Canada for more than 30 years before he was removed in December, 2015 because of criticisms that the clinic had been practising conversion therapy on young people who identify as transgender.

A review was launched.

The review found that the clinic focused on intensive assessment and treatment, despite current practice favouring "watchful waiting," and the education and support of parents in accepting their child's gender expression. (...)
In Dr. Zucker's view, it sparked a fear that the field of gender dysphoria – where he says there remains many urgent and unanswered clinical and theoretical questions – has been "poisoned by politics."

"I think that conflation with politics has made it very difficult for many people in the field to say what they really think," he said. "And I think that's really sad, that in a field where there are so many important issues to discuss and work on, that really bright people feel intimidated."

"I think the term conversion therapy is incredibly inflam-

---

25 Sally Robertson, "Hundreds of trans people regret changing their gender, says trans activist," *News Medical, Life Sciences*, October 7, 2019.

matory," he said. "I think it's been inappropriately expro-
priated from the original use of the term, where it was
directed at very conservative, religiously motivated clini-
cians or pastoral counsellors who were seeing, primarily,
homosexual men who didn't want to be gay. There were
lots of problems in trying to offer treatment to change an
adult's sexual orientation – we know that's a very dubious
proposition. But to apply [the term] to [treating] a three-
year-old child with gender dysphoria, in my opinion, is an
absurd comparison."[26]

Physician and former associate professor at Brown University, Lisa Littman, lost her job over a paper she wrote about
the sudden increase in female adolescents in her social network
who were coming out as transgender boys.

Until recently, the incidence of gender dysphoria was
thought to be rare, affecting an estimated one in 10,000
people in the U.S. While the exact number of trans-identi-
fying adolescents (or adults, for that matter) is unknown,
in the last decade or so, the number of youth seeking
treatment for gender dysphoria has spiked by over 1,000
percent in the U.S.; in the U.K., it's jumped by 4,000 percent. The largest youth gender clinic in Los Angeles reportedly saw 1,000 patients in 2019. That same clinic, in
2009, saw about 80.

Curious about what was happening, Littman surveyed
about 250 parents whose adolescent children had announced they were transgender — after never before
exhibiting the symptoms of gender dysphoria. Over 80
percent of cases involved girls; many were part of friend
groups in which half or more of the members had come
out as trans. Littman coined the term "rapid-onset gender
dysphoria" to describe this phenomenon. She posited that
it might be a sort of social contagion, not unlike cutting
or anorexia, both of which were endemic among teenage

---

26 Molly Hayes, "Doctor fired from gender identity clinic says he feels
'vindicated' after CAMH apology, settlement," *The Globe and Mail*, October
7, 2018.

girls when I was in high school in the '90s.

In August 2018, Littman published her results in a paper called "Rapid-Onset Gender Dysphoria in Adolescents and Young Adults: A Study of Parental Reports" in the journal *PLOS One*. Littman, the journal, and Brown University were pummeled with accusations of transphobia in the press and on social media. In response, the journal announced an investigation into Littman's work. Several hours later, Brown University issued a press release denouncing the professor's paper.[27]

This uptick sounds very much like a culturally acquired psychosis affecting one particular group, feeding on itself.

Futhermore, how did we get to a place where we state unequivocally that one cannot change one's sexual orientation? If a man loves a man, or a woman loves a woman, there is no "conversion" therapy that can possibly change that; yet, we are now promoting that one can change one's sex at will.

So, It's All About Feelings

I was under the impression that the Scopes Monkey Trial had settled the difference between science and belief. There were those who stated unequivocally that God created the earth in six days, and all creatures upon it, including man and woman—separate and distinct from the animal kingdom. Science said otherwise, and science won the day: we are descended from the ape family.

We are returning to a world where feelings and belief are superseding rationality and science, and that is a dangerous world. It is a world with no absolute right or wrong. A malignant morality. A morality based on feelings. There was a time when we knew that there were two sexes—male and female. Men have a penis. Women have a vagina. I believe that used to be taught in health class. We knew that there was a spectrum of male and female behaviour: feminine men and manly women.

---

27 Katie Herzog, "Med Schools Are Now Denying Biological Sex," opt. cit.

We also knew that some people liked to cross-dress. They were called transvestites. Now, it has always been easier for a woman to dress like a man than a man like a woman, but the possibility was always available. Perhaps we are living through Transvestite 2.0.

Today, if you feel like a woman, you are one. If you feel like a man, you are one. Damn the old-world science. This is "woke" science, part of social justice ideology. It is a refusal to accept the idea that we can be different but equal, in value, not necessarily in abilities.

Not too long ago, women athletes were thrown out of the Olympics for taking steroids, as they unfairly enhanced their abilities. Now we have boys who say they are girls winning in women's sports. As Andrew Sullivan wrote::

> There is no question that developing as a biological male under the influence of testosterone substantially improves athletic performance, even if subsequent T levels are suppressed. Including someone in the female category who was biologically male until a couple of years before the contest gives her a real advantage, however suppressed her current T levels are.[28]

However, the Court of Arbitration for Sport (CAS) declared:

> A woman in sport is anyone whose legal identity is female—whether they personally identify as such or not—and who has testosterone (T) levels in the female range.[29]

Can we not use that definition for all males and females? A little "fair" to pair with "equitable?"

If there is one thing that we as human beings must be able to say, without hesitation, is that the sex of an individual is determined by a pair of sex chromosomes. Females typically have

---

28   Andrew Sullivan, "Who Should Be Allowed to Compete in Women's Sports?" *New York Magazine Intelligencer*, May 10, 2019.

29   Doriane Lambelet Coleman, "A Victory for Female Athletes Everywhere," *Quillette*, May 3, 2019.

two of the same kind of sex chromosomes (XX), and are called the homogametic sex. Males typically have two different kinds of sex chromosomes (XY), and are called the heterogametic sex.

Usually, someone who has female body parts has two X chromosomes, and someone who has male body parts has an X and a Y chromosome. Currently, about 1 in 200 people identifies as transgender in the United States. That is 1.4 million people and growing.

There are no medical tests that can be done to know if someone is transgender, although there are some anomalies found very rarely in the sex chromosomes.

> For example, some people may have XXY, and some people may have one X or three X's. These are genetic conditions, which means sometimes having these chromosome differences can result in medical complications.

> Typically, if someone has a Y chromosome, no matter how many X's or Y's, they have the body parts of a boy. If someone doesn't have a Y chromosome, they have the body parts of a girl. About 1 in 1,600 people may have one of these sex chromosome differences.

> Now this is important: having differences in sex chromosomes doesn't mean that someone is transgender. Because remember, being transgender has more to do with how someone feels.[30]

This brings me back to Meghan Murphy, who gave a speech called "Gender Identity: What Does It Mean For Society, The Law and Women?" at a public library in Toronto, Canada. It was hosted by a group called Radical Feminists Unite. Murphy is a Vancouver journalist who has taken a feminist approach to everything from prostitution and pornography to hipster trends, anti-rape advertising and trigger warnings. She stated, "If you're born male, you remain male for life." She also said that

---

30 Kim Zayhowski, "Is being transgender related to having different sex chromosomes?" *The Tech Interactive*, December 5, 2017.

the "trans-activist movement has made for the erasure of women."[31] This was considered blasphemy by the politically correct left. According to Denise Balkissoon, a journalist at *The Globe and Mail* in Canada:

> Whatever the dictionary definition of 'woman' might read, it's always been an evolving, contentious term.
> (...)
> Womanhood isn't defined by femininity, race or class.
> (...)
> Ms. Murphy has earned notoriety through her blog, *Feminist Current*, on which she regularly declares who is and is not an adult woman with the right to define their own life.
> (...)
> True feminism seeks everyone's safety.[32]

Woman is an evolving contentious term? Well, maybe when it comes to her position in society, but biologically?

Balkissoon went on to write "such tensions may never be fully resolved, as 'woman' has never been a static category—spare me discussions of biology, unless you've abandoned your infertile and menopausal loved ones."[33]

That anyone would compare a woman—an absolute regarding sex chromosomes—who is infertile or menopausal with a made up "woman," that is, a man who claims to be a woman, takes us back to the Scopes Monkey Trial.

It's biology, not belief.

According to Balkissoon, Ms. Murphy would "rather make childish lists of who she thinks is and isn't a woman. Her purported feminism is hollow, made up of fear and meanness rather than a true desire for freedom."[34]

The insanity of it all. Childish lists of who is and is not

---

31 Liam Casey, "Hundreds protest controversial Toronto library event featuring Meghan Murphy," *The Canadian Press*, October 29, 2019.

32 Denise Balkissoon, "The targeting of other women shows Meghan Murphy is no feminist," *The Globe and Mail*, October 28, 2019.

33 Ibid.

34 Ibid.

a woman? If there is one thing that we as human beings must be able to say is that females have XX chromosomes and that a man has XY.

Outliers draw attention. We are allowing, if not promoting, outliers to take charge of our discourse. It's like making life and death medical decisions based on some anecdotes.

This is a true story about a woman who became a man but kept his/her uterus and had sex and got pregnant. Why is a man getting pregnant? How manly does she feel that she/he keeps her/his uterus? And how can you be living your "truth" as a man if you have a menstrual cycle?

> Freddy McConnell [a woman who felt like a man but kept its uterus and gave birth] wanted to be registered as "father" or "parent."

> But a High Court judge in Britain ruled the status of "mother" was afforded to a person who carries and gives birth to a baby.[35]

The last time I checked, women gave birth because they have the uterus, the garden into which the seed is planted by the penis from the man.

> The judge said while Mr. McConnell's gender was recognised by law as male, his parental status of "mother" derives from the biological role of giving birth.

> Mr. McConnell was a single parent, who was born a woman but now lived as a man following surgery. He was biologically able to get pregnant and gave birth to a baby boy, but had legally become a man by the time of the birth.[36]

But he wanted to be a man. So why did he have a baby? Isn't that a woman "feeling" thing?

---

35 "'Seahorse' transgender man loses challenge to be named father," *BBC News*, September 25, 2019.

36 Ibid.

I am a hospital chaplain. I have visited patients in the psychiatric ward. These particular people, men, believed they were Jesus Christ. They *knew* they were Jesus Christ. And because we knew they were not Jesus Christ, we kept them in the psychiatric ward as we helped them find their way back to themselves. But a man says he is a woman or a woman says she is a man and we are off and running to assist them in their hormone therapy and body mutilation. Does this make sense to you? Scientific sense?

This is insanity and we are permitting it. I fear what is next. Don't laugh that off. Did you ever think that doctors would agree that a male could become a female? There was a time, not that long ago, when people who had these concerns were treated for mental unwellness. Like the men who believed they were Jesus.

One might ask, how does a woman becoming a man get pregnant? Here is the answer.

> While testosterone generally blocks ovulation, trans men can get pregnant while taking it, particularly if they are not taking it regularly.
>
> It's just one example of the misinformation and discouragement transgender men say they face from the medical establishment when they decide to get pregnant—a problem advocates and experts blame on a lack of training and research around transgender health care, as well as doctors' biases.
> (...)
> In Australia, where government agencies began tracking both sex and gender in official records in 2013, 54 transgender men gave birth in 2014, And a Dutch study published in the journal Human Reproduction in 2011 found that a majority of trans men reported wanting families.
> (...)
> A recently published case study described a transgender man who went to an emergency room with severe abdominal pain — but doctors were slow to realize that he was pregnant and in danger. The man delivered a stillborn

baby several hours later.[37]

The doctors were slow to realize that HE was pregnant! Dear God: Whatever happened to science? It is all about belief. I think we are living in the Twilight Zone. Consider this custody battle:

> The parents of [a] 7-year-old have been locked in a bitter, public feud that sparked outrage among transgender advocates and Texas politicians alike. Anne Georgulas and Jeffrey Younger have been at odds about how to care for their child, who was assigned male at birth and whom Georgulas claims to be transgender. Younger disagrees.[38]

We don't let seven-year-old children stay home alone, but it's okay to let them decide what hormone treatment is for them? Do they know the purpose of hormones at age seven? And what about waiting until puberty when the secondary hormones come through? More testosterone is released. And the release of these hormones might influence the structure and function of the developing human brain. Nature just might take its course, if we let her. (Or, is it him or they?)

Letting children make these decisions—anyone making these decisions—can only happen when we walk away from science. Sex is assigned at birth based on… wait for it… genitalia.

> And predicting whether a prepubescent child will grow up to be transgender is difficult, said Jason Rafferty, a pediatrician and psychiatrist.
>
> (…)
>
> Most medical and psychological professionals agree that affirming children is the best approach for children with gender dysphoria, said Paul Mitrani, clinical director and

---

37 Julie Compton, "Trans dads tell doctors: 'You can be a man and have a baby,'" *NBC News*, May 19, 2019.

38 Lateshia Beachum, "Two parents disagree over whether their 7-year-old is transgender. Now they share custody," *The Washington Post*, October 29, 2019.

child and adolescent psychiatrist at the Child Mind Institute in New York.

> "Affirming is just saying, 'This is who you are right now,'" Mitrani said. "You're not trying to push them one way or another."
> (...)
> Hormone suppressants, which prevent the gonads from creating sex hormones, stop puberty, give families more time to decide about medical courses of action and can delay the stress that a developing body can cause a gender dysphoric teen, said Mitrani.[39]

The gender dysphoric, however, tend to demand "affirmation:"

> People with gender dysphoria may allow themselves to express their true selves and may openly want to be affirmed in their gender identity. They may use clothes and hairstyles and adopt a new first name of their experienced gender. Similarly children with gender dysphoria may express the wish to be of the opposite gender and may assert they are (or will grow up to be) of the opposite gender. They prefer, or demand, clothing, hairstyles and to be called a name of the opposite gender. (Medical transition is only relevant at and after the onset of puberty.)[40]

The American Psychiatric Association as stated the following:

> For children, cross-gender behaviors may start between ages 2 and 4, the same age at which most typically developing children begin showing gendered behaviors and interests. Gender atypical behavior is common among young children and may be part of normal development. Children who meet the criteria for gender dysphoria may or may not continue to experience it into adolescence and adulthood. Some research shows that children who

---

39 Ibid.

40 "What Is Gender Dysphoria?" *Now Comment*, undated. https://nowcomment.com/documents/135316/combined?embedded=true.

had more intense symptoms and distress, who were more persistent, insistent and consistent in their cross-gender statements and behaviors, and who used more declarative statements ("I am a boy (or girl)" rather than "I want to be a boy (or girl)") were more likely to become transgender adults.[41]

J.K. Rowling, a woman attacked for sharing her views on transgenderism, wrote: "I've been forced to the unhappy conclusion that an ethical and medical scandal is brewing. I believe the time is coming when those organizations and individuals who have uncritically embraced fashionable dogma, and demonized those urging caution, will have to answer for the harm they've enabled."[42]

So what is the hurry? Why are young children encouraged to think they are in the wrong body?

Your daughter is about to go off to university. She will be in a dorm. Girls only. The university picks the roommates. She discovers her roommate is a boy—well, now he is a girl, because he feels that way, but not committed enough to have his penis removed. Your daughter is not comfortable with this roommate. Does she have the right to say no? Should she have the right to say no? What would a human rights tribunal say?

Perhaps the time has come to talk about science versus belief, and fair versus equitable.

I end this chapter with a story about a prince and a rooster, "The Rooster Prince," written by Rebbe Nachman of Breslov, born 1772 in the Ukraine:

> There once was a prince who thought he was a rooster. His father and mother, the king and queen, were devastated when the prince entered the banquet hall one evening and announced, "I am no longer a prince, but a rooster!"

41   "What is Gender Dysphoria?" American Psychiatric Association, undated. https://www.psychiatry.org/patients-families/gender-dysphoria/what-is-gender-dysphoria.

42   Statement from J.K. Rowling regarding the Robert F Kennedy Human Rights Foundation Ripple of Hope Award, *JKRowling.com.* August 27, 2020.

and retreated beneath the dinner table, squawking like a rooster and picking up crumbs from the banquet hall floor. He refused to wear clothes, speak in human language, or eat with utensils.

For weeks and weeks, the king and queen tried with no success to convince their son that indeed he was not a rooster but a great prince! They called upon their community members to help, but no one could convince the prince that he was actually not a rooster. Finally, the king and queen called upon their trusted rabbi for advice.

The rabbi arrived to the banquet hall, crawled underneath the table, and perched next to the prince who thought he was a rooster. He clucked alongside the young rooster-prince, and they pecked at crumbs on the floor in unison. "I see that you want to be a rooster" the rabbi said, "but you know that you can still be a rooster and wear clothes." "I can?" the young prince replied, and the rabbi nodded. So the prince donned his princely robes once again. The rabbi told the rooster-prince that he could also remain a rooster and speak in human language, so he began to speak again. Finally, the rabbi said that he could still be a rooster even if he ate with utensils, so he sat up at the table alongside his family and community and proceeded to eat with a fork and knife.

The prince ate like a human, spoke like a human, and dressed like a human, but even with this outward appearance, he knew forever in his heart, that he was still a rooster.[43]

---

43 See: "The Rooster Prince," *Wikipedia*, https://en.wikipedia.org/wiki/The_Rooster_Prince#:~:text=The%20Rooster%20Prince%2C%20also%20sometimes,of%20stories%20by%20Rebbe%20Nachman.

20
Freedom of Expression Under Attack: Abuse of Language

Restriction of free thought and free speech is the most dangerous of all subversions. It is the one un-American act that could most easily defeat us. —Justice William O. Douglas[1]

ACCORDING TO Freedom House in 2019, "[F]reedom of expression has come under sustained attack, both through assaults on the press and encroachments on the speech rights of ordinary citizens."[2] Amy Lai, lawyer and author of *The Right to Parody*, a book on free speech and higher education, wrote:

> [F]reedom of speech has long been held as a fundamental right in the Western world. The view that free speech enables a "marketplace of ideas," often used with reference to John Stuart Mill's *On Liberty*, has its roots in a number of earlier works. For example, Enlightenment philosopher John Locke contended that freedom of conscience is an inalienable right in all humans, which, when guided by

---

1 "The One Un-American Act," Speech to the Author's Guild Council in New York, on receiving the 1951 Lauterbach Award, December 3, 1952.

2 Freedom House Report: *Democracy in Retreat: Freedom in the World,* 2019. pg. 7. https://freedomhouse.org/sites/default/files/Feb2019_FH_FITW_2019_Report_ForWeb-compressed.pdf.

reason, enables them to resist state coercion and pursue the truth. Free speech is essential not only to the pursuit of truth but also to democratic governance. Twentieth-century philosopher John Rawls considered free speech to be one of the basic liberties that enables citizens to participate in the lawmaking in a democracy. For moral philosopher Immanuel Kant, it is congenial to the self-development of individuals as much as it is important for a functional society.[3]

Note the statement: "Free speech is essential not only to the pursuit of truth but also to democratic governance." This freedom of speech is biblical. It was the prophet Jeremiah who died for the right to freedom of speech. Shall we allow the "Woke Progressives" to destroy 3500 years of that freedom?

Jasmin Zine, professor of sociology & the Muslim Studies Option at Wilfrid Laurier University, is an education consultant who has developed award-winning curriculum materials that address Islamophobia and anti-Muslim racism and has worked with the Office for Democratic Institutions and Human Rights at the Organization for Security and Cooperation in Europe (ODHIR/OSCE), the Council of Europe and the United Nations Educational, Scientific and Cultural Organization (UNESCO) on developing international guidelines for educators and policy-makers on combating Islamophobia and discrimination against Muslims. She is part of the *Islamophobia Research and Documentation Project*, an initiative designed to buttress the claim that Muslims are targets of wholesale discrimination and harassment in the West. She gave a keynote speech, "Islamophobia, Anti- Muslim Racism, and the Weaponizing of Free Speech," at The Road Traveled: 9th Annual International Islamophobia Conference, held at the University of California, Berkeley.[4] She is hard at work defending Islam as

---

3 Amy Lai, "On campus, unpopular views also deserve a platform," *The Globe and Mail,* May 27, 2019.

4 UC Berkeley, Center for Race and Gender, The Road Traveled: 9th Annual International Islamophobia Conference. https://www.crg.berkeley.edu/events/the-road-traveled-9th-annual-international-islamophobia-con-

it spreads throughout the West, by invoking the term "Islamophobia." Zine defines Islamophobia as "fear and hatred of Islam and Muslims that translates into individual, ideological and systemic forms of oppression."[5]

Pay attention to the language that she employs in the title of her speech: "Anti-Muslim Racism." Racism? The greatest accomplishment by the #IslamophobiaIndustry is the Orwellian twisting of language. Turning a religion, an ideology, into a race. Shall we turn Christianity into a race, too? We have worked hard to remove attacks on people based on race. One is born into one's race. It is not a choice. One cannot opt out of race.

To push the narrative that Islam is a race silences all discussion. This abuse of language is not an accident. In 2017, sociologist, writer and Montreal-based activist Dalila Awada, speaking to the Canadian Union of Public Employees, said:

> The first step to combatting Islamophobia is to recognize it as racism. Anti-Muslim racism shows itself in different ways, whether it is physical or verbal aggression or a family not being able to rent an apartment because the man's name is Mohammed and not Mark.

> We need to go beyond words like diversity and dialogue, as if they are magic formulas that solve all problems.[6]

Cancel culture is following in the footsteps of Islamophobia or vice versa.

If you are a professor who does not believe in made up pronouns, like Jordan Peterson, an academic psychologist, your career will be destroyed and the bullies of woke will try to cancel you as a human being as well. Professor Peterson's crime was refusing to abide by the Canadian law, Bill C-16, that appeared to make it mandatory to use their preferred pronouns when ad-

---

ference/.

5 Barbara Kay, "How academics portray Islam as a 'victim' of oppression — even as they defend violent Islamists," *National Post*, April 18, 2017.

6 "Society must fight Islamophobia, says Awada" *Canadian Union for Public Employees*, October 5, 2017.

dressing transgender individuals in class.

> [The year] 2016 was a "big year for transgender pronouns
> — in January of that year, the American Dialect Society
> officially anointed "they" as the gender-neutral pronoun
> to be used when addressing an individual whose pre-
> ferred pronoun is yet unknown. This decision was made
> up by 334 professionals in language fields, including ety-
> mologists, linguists, and grammarians." This is disfigured
> language.
> (...)
> Anne Curzan, English professor of the University of
> Michigan, stated in the New York Times: 'We've seen a
> lot of attention this year [2016] to people who are identi-
> fying out of the gender binary.' And the trans movement
> only truly picked up steam in the early '10s, with vocal
> advocates such as Laverne Cox and Caitlin Jenner. Young
> people were now asserting their preferred pronouns on
> university campuses.[7]

And that preference is making waves on campuses—places of higher learning. A university in Pennsylvania warned its
students that "action could be taken" if they fail to use their
classmates' preferred pronouns:

> The Point Park University student body recently received
> an email from the school's Office of Equity and Inclu-
> sion highlighting its Misgendering, Pronoun Misuse, and
> Deadnaming Policy. According to the correspondence,
> a copy of which was obtained by Campus Reform, 'any
> individual who has been informed of another person's
> gender identity, pronouns, or chosen name is expected
> to respect that individual... any violation, which in this
> instance applied to misgendering, misuse of pronouns,
> or incorrectly using someone's deadname when you are
> aware of their preferred name and pronouns,' could result
> in 'a similar action to any act of discrimination against

---

7 Justin Brown, "Why Jordan Peterson won't refer to transgender people by
their preferred pronouns," *Ideapod*, undated, 2018.

students on campus.'[8]

According to psychotherapist Julie Mencher, "I think we, and particularly young people, increasingly view gender not as a given, but as a choice, not as a distinction between male and female, but as a spectrum, regardless of what's 'down there'. Many claim that gender doesn't even exist."[9]

Peterson's stance has more to do with free speech than transgender issues. Peterson believes this is an issue of free speech, comparing state-regulated language to the practices of the Nazis, the Soviet Union and Orwell's classic *1984*. He understood the repercussions of speaking out. "The personal consequences of objecting are huge. The effect of my objection on society is miniscule. The risk isn't worth it." He argued that he and his like-minded colleagues were paralyzed by the introduction of these pronouns, and instead of using them, he simply ignored them. Until his refusal led to his termination. And he spoke. Peterson stated: "I'm not going to cede linguistic territory to post-modernist neo-Marxists."[10]

He faces a strong enemy. Diversity, inclusion and equity (DIE) are affecting our universities, the very places that used to seek out our best minds, the visionaries. As Philip Carl Salzman wrote:

[U]nder the label "diversity, inclusion, and equity," students, professors, staff, and administrators are treated in admissions, funding, hiring, and benefits not according to their ability to do the assigned job, but according to their sex, race, sexuality, ethnicity, and disability.[11]

---

8 Zoe Papadakis, "University Threatens Action Against Students Using Wrong Pronouns," *Newsmax*, September 23, 2021.

9 Justin Brown, "Why Jordan Peterson won't refer to transgender people by their preferred pronouns," op cit.

10 Ibid.

11 Philip Carl Salzman, "How 'Inclusion' in Canadian Universities Becomes Exclusion," *The Epoch Times*, March 27, 2021.

We walk on dangerous ground when we attack language.

21
The War of All Against All

When people are forced to remain silent when they are being told the most obvious lies, or even worse when they are forced to repeat the lies themselves, they lose once and for all their sense of probity... A society of emasculated liars is easy to control.
—Theodore Dalrymple

W<small>E ARE BEING</small> attacked by a fifth column in America: the Progressives and their apostles, Black Lives Matter and Critical Race Theory, seek to undermine our attachment to empiricism, reason and the scientific method. It feels as if the whirlwind of the Norse god Wotan, the god of irrationality, has re-emerged. He is a god with little concern for justice. Throughout history, his worshippers have sought prestige, honor and nobility rather than justice, fairness or respect for law and convention. They are forever ready to fight "the war of all against all."

This left-wing Progressive ideology is undermining the foundational documents of America and the West, based on the Judeo-Christian ethic, which was born 3500 years ago in a desert in the Middle East. This ethic was revealed so that anyone could take up its call to spiritual and intellectual freedom. America's Founding Fathers based the Constitution on the teachings of the Hebrew Bible, the blueprint for democracy. It is an ethic, a culture that honours the majority while protecting

217

the individual, and thus the minority, as well. This ethic belongs to no country and every country which embraces freedom. It is an ideology that changed us from tribal societies, incapable of caring for people outside the tribe, into a culture that teaches that all people are born with equal intrinsic value. The ethic inculcates the belief that all life is sacred, and we have moral agency. We each have free will that demands of us that we choose, and choose wisely, between good and evil from the understanding it bequeaths to us. It is the only ethic that not only promotes freedom but demands it of its citizens, because freedom can be frightening and so easily relinquished.

Fear from the bullying tactics by the Left has silenced too many of us. And the Left has counted on fear to keep its opponents silent. They counted on teachers and parents and hard-working Americans to be silent. They counted on politicians to be silent. They counted on the word "racist" to silence all dissent.

We have a lot to learn from the lessons taught by Manning Johnson (1908 – 1959) as shared by Bill Bowman:

> Few people have heard of Manning Johnson (1908 – 1959). He was a unique, intelligent and influential Black man from New York who was successfully recruited by the American Communist Party at a very young age. His job as a communist community organizer was to convince Black Americans that white America would continue to suppress them and that their lives would be so much better under a Socialist/Marxist/Communist government. He was very good at his job, and rose fast through the ranks of the Communist Party until he held one of the highest positions on their National Committee. There he was trained to disrupt cities and towns, organize mobs, incite riots, attack police to include how to strategically and tactfully "throw a brick and hide." Does all this sound familiar? It should.
>
> Miraculously and mostly because of his Christian upbringing, Johnson had a revelation and realized the communist strategies, tactics and lies were not at all beneficial

to Black Americans and only causing more hardship and suppression. He saw the deception and how the rejection of traditional American values and contempt of Christianity lowered the value of humanity and quality of life. This is when he turned government witness opposing Socialism and Communism.

...[L]ike Dr. King, Manning ultimately gave his life spreading the word, educating and warning Black Americans of the cruelty and diabolical strategies used by the angry liberal left in their attempt to hand over the U.S. to the Socialist and Communist Party. This was Johnson's mission and passion until his untimely death in 1959.

Johnson testified before Congress several times about the Communist plot to take over America. His testimony is a matter of record. His testimony and the threats to our democracy are as relevant today as they were then. After he left the Communist Party in 1940, he authored an amazing book titled *Color, Communism and Common Sense*. This book could have been written yesterday. He details his experiences with communist leaders and the liberal left conspiracy and the sordid tactics they use. Ending democracy and capitalism will never bring us peace and prosperity. No one can name even one country where socialism has been successful.[1]

We have traveled this road before. We watched as Germans gave into Hitler's demands because they were too scared to disobey Nazi laws. Looking back today, when once again cancel culture has frightened people into silence, I think we have a better understanding of the German people under Hitler. Fear leads to submission!

And, sadly, we watched and have forgotten how Jews, out of fear, allowed themselves to believe the lies of the Nazis. They allowed themselves to believe that all would be well if they just followed orders. In Hungary, Adolf Eichmann convinced the

---

1 Bill Bowman, "Manning Johnson: American author and patriot," *Up & Coming Weekly,* September 23, 2020.

Jewish Council of Budapest to trust him and keep the Jewish community calm, not to worry. So the Jewish leadership told the people not to worry and cooperate. Soon, Jews were wearing the Jewish star on their clothes. Then telephones were taken away and the shops were closed, appliances were taken away. And yet, the final letter sent out by the Budapest Jewish Council exhorted the Jews to comply with all regulations to avoid a disaster. Despite everything that was taking place, fear kept the leadership from speaking truth. And in the end, as Kati Marton wrote in her book, *Wallenberg*,[2] soon the gendarmes ran out of things to take away, so they took people to Auschwitz.

Perhaps we have had it "too good." Too many generations of people have been handed freedom, without a fight, and they have taken that freedom for granted. They have no idea what it means to fight for one's freedom, and just as importantly, the freedom of others.

Echoes of Niemöller

Martin Niemöller was a prominent Protestant pastor who emerged as an outspoken public foe of Adolf Hitler and spent the last seven years of Nazi rule in concentration camps, despite his ardent nationalism. He is remembered for his poem about loss of freedom from silence.

> First they came for the socialists, and I did not speak out—because I was not a socialist.
> Then they came for the trade unionists, and I did not speak out— because I was not a trade unionist.
> Then they came for the Jews, and I did not speak out—because I was not a Jew.
> Then they came for me—and there was no one left to speak for me.

That's how submission works.

What does it take for us to learn that being quiet never

---

2 Kati Marton, *Wallenberg: The Incredible True Story of the Man Who Saved the Jews of Budapest,* Arcade; Centenary Edition, October 1, 2011.

works out well?

When will we learn that fighting for one's own freedom is selfish; rather, it is fighting for the freedom of others that is the better part of valour?

A free society depends on the dignity of dissent. John Stewart Mill, the most famous and influential British philosopher of the nineteenth century, believed that freedom includes the right to voice opinions that dissent from the majority view of a society at a given time. That is the only way we correct error—by allowing dissent of voice. In Roman law, there is a principle of justice which says, *audi alteram partem*, which means justice depends on the ability to listen to the other side. As Rabbi Sacks has said:

> When one side is silent, there is neither freedom nor justice.[3]

3 Rabbi Jonathan Sacks, "In Defence of Religious Liberty," Acceptance speech at the Becket Fund for Religious Liberty, May 15, 2014.

22

We Are Our Stories

Cancel our words, cancel our stories, and we are bereft.

ALLAN BLOOM, author of *The Closing of the American Mind*, 1987, wrote that many of us find our purpose and our intellectual and spiritual connection to the world through the stories and wisdom of the Bible, unlike many people who live with "an open-ended future and the lack of a binding past" and are in "a condition like that of the first men in the state of nature, spiritually unclad, unconnected, isolated, with no inherited or unconditional connection with anything or anyone."[1]

The West is at war. A battle between two cultures that are diametrically opposed to each other. We are witnessing an attack on our values from Progressive bullies pushing Critical Race Theory and devaluing the family. This is leading us into a mental health breakdown.

I believe this war is only possible because we stopped teaching the Judeo-Christian ethic that underpins freedom. Niall Ferguson wrote in 2011: "Maybe the ultimate threat to the West comes from our own lack of understanding and faith in our own cultural heritage."[2]

---

1 Allan Bloom, *The Closing of the American Mind*, Simon & Schuster, 1987, p. 87.

2 Niall Ferguson, *Civilization: The West and the Rest*, Penguin Books, 2011, p. 255.

The West promotes freedom, free will, free speech, the knowledge that one is the subject of one's destiny, because one has the right and the obligation to choose his or her own path. This new culture, what writer Wesley Yang refers to as "the successor ideology," is a culture which takes us back to a time of artificially designed hierarchies, and which promotes the belief that one is the object of one's fate, hampered and held back by race, colour, creed, religion or sexual orientation. This is a culture which promotes standing on the shoulders of giants, not to rise up and reach for the stars but bury them in the dust, erasing the very existence of earlier generations in fits of self-righteous pique.

Cancel culture is the Siamese twin of progressivism: "Given the predilection to progress, the past is viewed as an inferior state of existence with various afflictions that wither away over time."[3]

Cancel culture has no use for the individual. Instead of uniting behind the social contract, the general will and the COMMON good, cancel culture is intent upon dividing us into competing tribes: divide and conquer. Cancel culture will never concede that we can be different, but equal. Rather, cancel culture promotes "othering," turning the "other" into something "lesser than" rather than different but equal. It may feel as if cancel culture hit us head on without mercy and little resistance, but it didn't. It has slowly infiltrated our culture with the sole purpose of destroying it. While Western Culture is firmly rooted in the Judeo-Christian ethic, cancel culture is firmly rooted in Critical Race Theory.

Cancel culture is in the business of "linguistic engineering." What words are correct and others that must be eviscerated. Wilhelm von Humboldt said in the eighteenth century:

> Language is, as it were, the external manifestation of the minds of the peoples. Their language is their soul, and

---

3 Bruce Frohnen, Jeremy Beer, Jeffery O. Nelson (Editors), *American Conservatism: An Encyclopedia*, Intercollegiate Studies Institute, 2006. Under "progressivism."

their soul is their language.[4]

In the twentieth century, Roland Barthes wrote:

> Man does not exist prior to language, either as a species or an individual. We never find a state where man is separated from language, which he then creates in order to 'express' what is taking place within him: it is language which teaches the definition of man, not the reverse.[5]

Barbara Hardy, British literary scholar, author, and poet wrote:

> We dream in narrative, daydream in narrative, remember, anticipate, hope, despair, believe, doubt, plan, revise, criticise, construct, gossip, learn, hate and love by narrative.[6]

More recently, poet Muriel Rukeyser wrote:

> The universe is made of stories, not atoms.[7]

Cancel our words, cancel our stories, and we are bereft. Alasdair MacIntyre wrote:

> Man is in his actions and practice as well as in his fictions essentially a story telling animal. It is through narratives that we begin to learn who we are and how we are called on to behave. Deprive children of stories you leave them unscripted anxious stutterers and their actions is in their words.[8]

---

4 Wilhelm von Humboldt, *On Language: On the Diversity of Human Language Construction and its Influence on the Mental Development of the Human Species,* Cambridge University Press, 1999.

5 Quoted in *On the Origin of Stories: Evolution, Cognition, and Fiction* by Brian Boyd, Belknap Press, 2010. p. 337.

6 Barbara Hardy, "An Approach Through Narrative," *Novel: A Forum on Fiction 2,* Duke University Press, 1968, p. 5.

7 Muriel Rukeyser, *The Speed of Darkness,* Random House, 1968.

8 Alasdair MacIntyre, *After Virtue: A Study in Moral Theory,* University of Notre Dame Press, 1981, p. 201.

Our children are being deprived, and the result is a rise in confusion and mental illness.

We are colluding in the spread of cancel culture with our silence, often out of fear. And that fear could lead to the downfall of our hard-fought way of life. I will repeat the words of the late, great journalist, George Jonas, who wrote: "Don't let Western civilization—the best and most humane form of civilization developed by mankind—perish by default."[9]

The fifth book of the Bible, Deuteronomy, implores us to: "Remember the days of old, consider the years of ages past."

The late Rabbi Sacks wrote:

> Moses warns the people – no less than fourteen times – *not to forget*. If they forget the past they will lose their identity and sense of direction and disaster will follow. Moreover, not only are the people commanded to remember, they are also commanded to hand that memory on to their children.
>
> This entire phenomenon represents a remarkable cluster of ideas: about identity as a matter of collective memory; about the ritual retelling of the nation's story; above all about the fact that *every one of us is a guardian of that story and memory*. It is not the leader alone, or some elite, who are trained to recall the past, but every one of us.
> (...)
> Narrative is at the heart of covenantal politics because it locates national identity in a set of historic events. The memory of those events evokes the values for which those who came before us fought and of which we are the guardians.
>
> A covenantal narrative is always inclusive, the property of all its citizens, newcomers as well as the native-born. It says to everyone, regardless of class or creed: this is who we are. It creates a sense of common identity that tran-

---

9 George Jonas, "The 10 Commandments of sending your troops to war," *National Post*, April 2, 2011.

scends other identities.[10]

Rabbi Sacks also wrote that we are bound by collective responsibility—to one another, to the past and future.

The greatest stories ever told are in the Bible. One does not need to be religious to see that the stories in the Bible are there to teach us how to be compassionate people in a compassionate society. The stories in the Bible tell us not to fear and that we must remember. The past is part of our present and the present will affect the future. "Remember the days of old; consider the generations long past. Ask your father and he will tell you, your elders, and they will explain to you." (Deut. 32:7)

We are our stories, our narratives. The question is which stories will we pass down to our children, grandchildren and all those who come after? Will we share the stories that contain the ethic that all people are born with equal intrinsic value, that all life is sacred, that we have free will? Will we teach that we are the subjects of our destiny and not the objects of fate? That we are to be measured by our character and not our innate characteristics? Or will we fall prey to Progressive cancel culture, Critical Race Theory and the propaganda from Black Lives Matter that is trying to divide us with an ethic that states that white people are oppressors and people of colour are victims, perpetual children who need to be protected?

Granted, we have not fulfilled the teachings of this Judeo-Christian ethic and its stories, but we are human, and humans will never be perfect, but we can strive for that perfection, for a world where race, color, creed and sexual orientation have no bearing on our way of life, where we are judged only by our deeds. Where all life is sacred. And we have the right and obligation to choose our path forward, because it is *not* pre-destined.

In this war of the words, what will it be? Will we succumb to Progressive bullies and the trail of mental illness they leave behind based on the narrative that the past is "an inferior state of

---

10   Rabbi Jonathan Sacks, "A Nation of Storytellers." https://mailchi.mp/ rabbisacks/ki-tavo-245360?e=507d358848.

existence with various afflictions that wither away over time?"[11] Or, will we go forward knowing the past is part of our present and can make us more compassionate and caring people?

What we learn from history is that we do not learn from history. — Georg Wilhelm Friedrich Hegel

---

11 Bruce Frohnen, et. al., op. cit.

A people without the knowledge of their past history, origin and culture is like a tree without roots. —Marcus Garvey

CPSIA information can be obtained
at www.ICGtesting.com
Printed in the USA
BVHW041130300822
645843BV00014B/446/J

9 781943 003631